Thought for the Day

Thought for the Day

Selections from BBC Radio 4

British Broadcasting Corporation

Published by the British Broadcasting Corporation
35 Marylebone High Street, London W1M 4AA
ISBN 0 563 12666 3
First published 1974

Printed in England
by Tonbridge Printers Ltd,
Tonbridge, Kent

Contents

Preface

This volume contains selections from the popular Radio 4 programme *Thought for the Day*. Each morning at 7.45 a speaker attempts to provide a very large audience with a thought, the germ of an idea, which, hopefully, will help them make more sense of the problems of daily life. There is probably no programme on the air today which receives more unsolicited letters and telephone calls than this! Overwhelmingly the comments are kind and favourable. We take this as a sign that though, inevitably, some speakers fail to 'reach' the listeners, many in fact do bring comfort and enlightenment.

It is to give those who want a more permanent record that this book of fifty talks has been compiled. The first part, *Random Thoughts*, is a selection from talks broadcast over the last eighteen months. The second part, *Learning to Live*, is made up of a five-week series given during Lent 1974.

As producers and, in this instance, editors of *Thought for the Day*, we take this opportunity of thanking all our contributors and listeners for their co-operation and their kindness.

PETER DE ROSA
DAVID WINTER
April 1974

Part One: Random Thoughts

Eternal Father

CLAUDE MUNCASTER

Sometimes when we sing hymns, we are so captivated by the tune we fail to notice how beautiful the words are. Take the words of 'Eternal Father':

Eternal Father, strong to save,
Whose arm hath bound the restless wave,
Who bidd'st the mighty ocean deep
Its own appointed limits keep;
O hear us when we cry to thee
For those in peril on the sea.

O Christ, whose voice the waters heard,
And hushed their raging at thy word,
Who walkedst on the foaming deep,
And calm, amid the storm, didst sleep;
O hear us when we cry to thee
For those in peril on the sea.

O Holy Spirit, who didst brood
Upon the waters dark and rude,
And bid their angry tumult cease,
And give, for wild confusion, peace;
O hear us when we cry to thee
For those in peril on the sea.

O Trinity of love and power,
Our brethren shield in danger's hour;
From rock and tempest, fire and foe,
Protect them wheresoe'er they go;
Thus evermore shall rise to thee,
Glad hymns of praise from land and sea.

Yes! I think that really must be my favourite hymn. I remember hearing it sung in a little church or chapel above Cadgewith on the Cornish coast on a morning after a wild night when the Cadgewith life-boat had been called out to a ship in distress. I knew most of the men. I'd heard them singing 'Eternal Father' on their way to football matches when I played 'goalie' for them. I'd heard them singing it on the Todden Rock in Cadgewith Cove on a summer's evening. I'd been out in the life-boat with those same men. It was only a practice, the sea being too rough for fishing. But I wished it had been the real thing and that we were really rowing out to save 'those in peril on the sea'.

What is this extraordinary call of the sea? Why be a trawlerman, for instance, risking his life in arctic weather when flying spray freezes on the top hamper and the weight of the ice makes the vessel liable to capsize? Is it inheritance? A desire for money? I can think of many softer jobs where the pay is higher but the work far less arduous and dangerous.

To the marine artist the sea offers a tremendous challenge because of its inconstancy of moods. I have seen it in so many of them from aloft in a sailing ship battling amid the savageries of the Horn to the same ship windless and immobile in an equatorial calm.

Through these experiences I became aware that, despite the changing effects, the sea, like all else in nature, is but obeying the divine laws. And as to Man, he cannot change the tides and the currents, or the fact that every seventh wave is the largest. If Man refuses to conform to law, he stands in great peril of being lost. He has built ships which float, ships made of skins, wood, iron or steel, and learnt to achieve something which at first seemed impossible. But if he follows the guidance of eternal law, humbly and industriously, and he believes, then *nothing* is impossible.

There is no better place to observe the vastness of the universe than at sea on a clear and starry night where there is an unimpeded view. To gaze up into that starlit dome of heaven and see those magnificent constellations, Orion's Belt, the Plough or the Southern Cross with their myriad starlight attendants, is to observe something of infinite beauty, but withal, something a little awe-inspiring. For up there is limitless space, and time without beginning and without end. There indeed is Eternity. And to be face to face with Eternity can make one feel incredibly small!

Yet, remember, however small Man is, however microscopic he is in view of the vastness of the universe, his life is supremely important; it is a gift he simply must not squander. For only Man can turn to his Creator and glorify him saying:

> Thus evermore shall rise to thee
> Glad hymns of praise from land and sea.

The Holiness of Beauty

C. A. JOYCE

I live in the Isle of Wight, and the motto on the Island's Coat of Arms is, 'All this beauty is of God'. Even today there is so much natural beauty that is inspiring and unbelievably lovely.

There is a hymn that bids us 'Worship the Lord in the beauty of holiness'. Very often I can get young people to understand that more clearly by asking them to *Worship the Lord in the Holiness of Beauty*. They find nothing difficult about that when they fall in love. It's a great pity if they lose it later on because there's no need to do so! The beautiful picture, the inspiration of lovely music and really good verse can and do lift up our hearts in ways we cannot explain. We are not overwhelmed by *the mathematics* of the sun and the rainbow, the song of birds, the loveliness of people. They are like the peace of God which passes all understanding, but no less real for all that.

Sometimes we say of people that they have beautiful characters. It could be that in them shines something of that holiness of beauty which Christ possessed. I'm reminded of a poem whose title I remember, but not its origin or its author. It's called 'The Living Christ':

> Not merely in the words you say, not only in the deeds confessed,
> But in the most unconscious way is Christ expressed.
> Is it a very saintly smile? A holy light upon your brow?
> Oh no! I felt his presence while you laughed just now.
> For me, 'twas not the truth you *taught*, to you so clear, to me so dim:
> But when *you* came, you straightway brought a sense of him.
> So from your life he beckons me, and from your heart his love is shed.
> Till I lose sight of you, and see the Christ instead.

When I look back on my life I can recall two small incidents which made a deep impression on me.

As a small boy I used to spend a month every year on my

grandfather's farm in Hampshire. At about six o'clock every morning I joined him for breakfast and then we went off to work often as day was breaking. One day we set off with two horses to plough. I had never heard the old man say anything about religion or about God, but on this particular morning we crested the brow of a hill as the sun rose in golden glory. My grandfather pulled up the horses and stood silent for a moment, and with a voice full of awe he said: 'God Almighty!' He saw in nature the holiness of beauty.

The second memory goes back to the years when I was the Headmaster of the Cotswold Approved School. We had one very difficult boy who did all he could to upset the Chaplain's work and sneer at religion and chapel services. In the school grounds I had a number of large aviaries housing lovely birds of glorious colours. All around there was an atmosphere of natural beauty and freedom. One evening I stood by an aviary in which were golden pheasants. One of the cock birds was walking up and down, displaying his beautiful colours in the late sunshine. The boy and I stood in silence for some minutes, and suddenly he said, 'Christ Almighty! How can people say there isn't a God?'

The Holiness of Beauty got through to him, indeed![1]

The Sabbath Minute

DAVID BLACKHALL

There are fourteen hundred and forty minutes in a day, just over half a million in a year, and one of them is now. There is no reason in the world why this minute should not belong to me. It can be mine to do what I like with, it can be yours to do what you like with.

[1]C. A. Joyce has developed this idea in *A Thought For The Week*, Lakeland Press, 1974.

I believe there's no salvation in beginning sentences with 'If only' or 'I wish', especially if they are tinged with wistful day-dreaming, but I'll do it this once. If only we could use one minute every day to stop the wheels from turning, the kind which go on and on by themselves; if only we could stop being buffeted by life for one fourteen-hundred-and-fortieth of the day, it would be better than travelling a thousand miles away from it all. The sad thing is that we can take our misery with us wherever we go, we can't escape from ourselves. Let me say what we *can* do.

We can make this minute our very own, we can hold it carefully in the palm of the hand, never, never by the scruff of the neck! We can be living our lives in this minute, instead of living yesterday again or worrying about to-morrow.

All the time we're awake – possibly when we're asleep, too – the human mind goes on churning, so I can't tell you to stop thinking. But it is something like that, because we can separate ourselves, just for this minute, from the mechanical process in the human computer which passes for thinking. We can find a resting-place, not a thousand miles away, but in ourselves, in the private sanctuary of our own understanding, which we can also take with us wherever we go. And when I need a prop to lean on, I call to mind a few lines from a poem with a very unpretentious title: Psalm 139.

> If I take the wings of the morning, and dwell in the uttermost parts of the sea, even there shall thy hand lead me and thy right hand shall hold me.
> If I say: Surely the darkness shall cover me; even the night shall be light about me.
> Yea, the darkness hideth not from thee but the night shineth as the day. The darkness and the light are both alike to thee.

Don't forget that there are other kinds of darkness besides the kind when the sun goes down or the lights fuse. This minute of choice is like standing between darkness and light, whether you want to go on ricocheting from event to event without stopping to take breath, or whether you want to be aware of yourself in this minute, your entire consciousness wide open to all the world and all its people, and everything quiet and still.

We've been given a Sabbath day, a time for ceasing, for standing aside. We can make for ourselves a Sabbath minute and there are fourteen hundred and forty chances every day. To separate ourselves from the immediate cares of the day, to find that private sanctuary in the Sabbath of the heart, is like opening a secret door, like walking through the storm and keeping dry.

It's one thing to snatch a minute for ourselves from the burdensome day but, for myself, I believe there would be little significance in the exercise unless I related it and myself to an everlasting minute in another dimension of time called Eternity.

Wordless Prayer

COLIN MORRIS

In the widest sense of the term, prayer is a universal human activity because man can never completely control either himself or the world in which he lives. He has mastered many of life's forces but he is still at the mercy of others, and so long as there is this gap between what man can do and what is done to him, he will have the urge to bridge it by hoping, rebelling, longing, wishing, despairing – by praying, in fact.

Prayer is the cry of our deepest needs, our innermost longings. Ask the average man if he has a prayer-life and he'll probably say no – sheepishly, defiantly or as a matter of complete indifference. Ask him if he has a life of desire and he'll tell you he has plenty of that, unless of course he tells you quite properly to mind your own business. So let's not play around with words. Desire *is* prayer. We who call ourselves religious often pray at two levels – there are the things we feel we ought to say, and deep beneath the level of our words are our clamant desires, our real demands on life, our wordless and often confused longings. These are the prayers that count.

The most elementary form of prayer, however, has nothing to do with asking God for things. It's wordless. It is simply letting go, resting back, floating like a tired swimmer, trusting that something or Someone will carry us when we can no longer carry whatever life piles on to us. And if you're like me, a teeth-grinding, tense individual with nerves as taut as violin-strings, a walking zoo of conflicting and roaring passions and emotions, then unless you can let go from time to time, you're likely to lose your sanity let alone your efficiency.

Now this sort of prayer doesn't require much faith – just enough to believe that there is at the heart of the world a core of stability; that it won't come apart at the seams unless we grimly try to hold it together. The Christian believes a lot more than that. But it's a beginning. Prayer is about letting go, relaxing, abandoning the role of Atlas who carried the world on his back, and allowing the world to carry us for a while.

Sheer irresponsibility! snorts the activist. We've got to take hold of life by the scruff of the neck and shake it like a terrier with a rat. Yet I've never met an activist who didn't concede the need for sleep, a period of passivity in which to recruit fresh strength for the fray. People who won't or can't let go are spiritual insomniacs, they fail to obey the essential rhythm of life, where rootage alternates with fruitage, activity with receptivity, work with rest. If sometimes you don't let go, you won't be able to hang on indefinitely. If you don't cultivate inner serenity, you'll be unable to stand up to outer frenzy.

Man's relationship to God isn't that of a beggar to an Eastern potentate, though you might think so from the form of some of our prayers. Man relates to God like a fish relates to water. The water supports, protects and sustains it even though the fish isn't conscious of the fact unless it finds itself flapping helplessly on dry land. God is our ultimate environment – as Paul put it, he is in all, through all, over all, and one might add, under all. So if you let go, you won't drop through the bottom of the world. According to the Psalmist, underneath are the everlasting arms – and they haven't dropped a catch yet.

When Hopeful in *Pilgrim's Progress* is half-way across the dark river, he calls back to his friend on the bank, 'Be of good cheer, my brother, for I feel the bottom and it is sound.'

Listen to these great words of reassurance given by the Psalmist about the unshakeable core at the heart of things:

> God is our refuge and strength, a very present help in time of trouble.
> Therefore we will not fear though the earth should change; though the mountains shake in the heart of the sea; though its waters roar and foam; though the mountains tremble with its tumult.
> Be still, and know that I am God. (Psalm 46: 1–10.)

Bright Visions on Dark Mornings

ROBERT BLACKLEDGE

Not everybody has *great* visions of what life is about. But everybody ought to have *some* vision. After all, there is a part for everyone to play. It may not *seem* much of a part, but if we don't play it, you can be sure *someone* will miss it. St Paul wrote:

> Be transformed by the renewal of your mind . . . For as in one body we have many members, and all the members do not have the same function, so we, though many, are one body in Christ, and individually members one of another. Having gifts that differ according to the grace given to us, let us use them: if prophecy, in proportion to our faith; if service, in our serving; he who teaches, in his teaching; he who exhorts in his exhortation ; he who contributes, in liberality; he who gives aid, with zeal; he who does acts of mercy, with cheerfulness. (Rom. 2: 2–8.)

St Paul insists there's a place and a part for all of us. Whatever we do is important to the welfare of the whole community. And this applies to people who are old, or ill or who have boring work to do. This truth is self-evident: if you're depressed, people around you get depressed, nerves get frayed, jobs get done badly. If you're cheerful, people take courage from you, get stirred by the thought that if you can be like that, they must tackle things with humour and even courage. It's our attitude that counts.

But what of the visions we hold, or once held? You all know the dreams one has as a child about the kind of job and life we shall be living in twenty years' time. You will probably, therefore, agree with me when I say it's a difficult time for older pupils at school at the moment. Exams may be just round the corner, and their future may hang on them. Others may be looking at possible careers. A vision of what life could be like will help them to organise, to plan – will motivate them. Without it, they may lose their way.

To some extent, we all have this problem. We may already feel we've lost our way, or simply that there is no way, no purpose in it.

I always remember being demobilised in May 1946, in York. I'd travelled all night by train from Swansea through Central Wales. It was early morning when I arrived in York, and I had plenty of time to wander round the empty streets, and to admire the outside of the minster and the streets of the lovely old city.

Suddenly, it struck me: the thought that now I was on my own. The protective cocoon which the army system had built round me for six years had been ripped away. Who was to help in the planning of my life?

I was bewildered, and stayed like that until half-way through my degree course. Then two years later, with the help of friends and work, I got back onto something like an even keel. And with a vision of the future. But this vision needed to be kept sharp. It needed to be challenged, and nurtured.

It's hard to keep visions alive on dull mornings. But it's just something that's got to be done. In some way, shape or form, we've got to keep a vision of our part, our usefulness to the human race in general, and to those around us in particular.

In that vision, we've usually seen ourselves as bestowers of justice and kindness, and succeeding through our courage and honesty. Well, keep it going. What's wrong with those things? We've reacted too much to the prophets of gloom, who say that honesty doesn't pay, that life is for the fittest. And this is where we need to say quite deliberately to ourselves: Forget it. Renew your mind, as St Paul says. We are necessary to one another. We are amazing people. All of us.

Unbridled Curiosity

GONVILLE FFRENCH-BEYTAGH

My theme is rash curiosity and I want to illustrate it by a passage from a favourite book, *Alice in Wonderland:*

> Alice was beginning to get very tired of sitting by her sister on the bank when suddenly a White Rabbit with pink eyes ran close by her. When the Rabbit actually took a watch out of its waistcoat-pocket and looked at it, and then hurried on, Alice started to her feet, for it flashed across her mind that she had never before seen a rabbit with either a waistcoat-pocket or a watch to take out of it and, burning with curiosity, she ran across the field after it and was just in time to see it pop down a large rabbit-hole under the hedge.
>
> In another moment down went Alice after it, never once considering how in the world she was to get out again.

Perhaps there was every excuse for Alice in the circumstances, but unbridled curiosity can do a great deal of harm. We are all extraordinarily curious about what other people think of us. 'Will this group, which I want to join, accept me as a friend?' 'Will I make an impression?' 'Am I popular?' 'Do people listen to me?' And then there is the curiosity which leads to a great deal of malicious gossip. You know what it's like when people are trying to fish for a bit more information. 'What is really going on between those two . . .?' 'Have you heard . . .?' 'Did you know . . .?'

Curiosity is also one of the main reasons why young people try drugs, 'never once considering', in Lewis Carroll's famous words, 'how in the world they are going to get out again'. They begin by wondering, 'What will happen if I do?' 'What is it like?' 'What will it do to me?' They find out soon enough, to their cost. And, of course, curiosity is responsible for a great deal of sexual aberration as well as ordinary sexual immorality. It is one of the reasons why a happily married – or apparently happily married man – will totally lose his head about some young girl. Or why an unmarried woman who is content and fulfilled in her own way of life will give herself a great deal of misery 'just to see what it's like'.

Anyway, Alice jumped in with both feet and she went down and down and found it all rather pleasant, as in fact it is, drifting slowly with the stream. Jesus said, 'Broad and easy is the path leading to destruction'. Broad and easy; just floating down. You remember that while Alice floated she passed shelves full of pleasant things and as she was particularly fond of orange marmalade, she took a lovely big jar of it off a shelf and opened it. But of course it was empty, as these things are. At least that was my experience when I lived that kind of life – pleasant and uncaring, but just empty.

When Alice got to the bottom she made a very soft landing on a pile of old leaves and that, of course, is one of the troubles with this kind of ordinary sin. The landing is so awfully soft that you just don't know when you have reached rock bottom. There are people who keep on saying, 'I'm not doing anybody any harm', but they are! By virtue of the fact that they are not doing anybody any good, they are harming themselves; and all their talents are going to waste. And, naturally, you never know *when* you are doing harm. Even a glance, or an offhand word, sometimes cuts to the quick. To say that you're not doing any harm is simply untrue.

The trouble is that the world and Jesus have different attitudes towards sin. The world says that sin is short and sharp and obvious. 'Adultery! Murder! Theft! Those are things that will get you to hell'. But it is not necessarily true. If you do that sort of thing, the chances are that you will be brought up, bang! And then you may repent. (Mind you, I am *not* recommending adultery and murder and theft as ways to God!)

My point is that the ordinary person just tends to drift and drift. He doesn't think that he is drifting downwards to rockbottom, but the Biblical fact of the matter is that this is what he is doing.

This is why Jesus says, 'Broad and easy is the road leading to destruction'. I am convinced that it is the little things, the things you hardly notice, which often matter most.

The Royal Wedding

THE ARCHBISHOP OF CANTERBURY

Need we ask what millions will be thinking about today? They will be thinking about turning on the TV so as to watch the Royal Wedding.

I shall be there in the Abbey, marrying Princess Anne and Captain Mark Phillips, and you'll see at the great moment just the three – the bridegroom, the bride and the Archbishop who marries them.

At that moment you'll be forgetting, and we'll be forgetting, the pageantry and splendour and be aware of the simplest thing in the world, that which happens at every wedding in any town or village in the land, 'I, Mark, take thee, Anne, to my wedded wife till death us do part'. 'I, Anne, take thee, Mark, to my wedded husband till death us do part'.

The Archbishop, like any priest in the land, declares them

man and wife together, and what tremendous words follow: 'Those whom God hath joined together, let no man put asunder'.

What will be *your* thought for the day? Well, say a prayer for them, that their marriage will be wonderfully happy, a marriage which keeps close to God. And if you are married, look back to your own wedding day and think of all the happiness you have had in your marriage since. And thank God for it. Renew now your gratitude to God, because His goodness is behind all the good things we have.

Then a more far-reaching thought. Millions today, watching and seeing and hearing, will be challenged to think again about what marriage really means, and what are its tremendous privileges and obligations. Today could have a deep effect on the people of this country.

There are too many marriages which fall short, marriages which get under strain, marriages indeed which break down – and why? Because in one way or another it isn't grasped that marriage is a great adventure in unselfishness, in sacrifice; an adventure with many hazards; an adventure of discovering more and more what are its sacrifices, and its joys. And that's the nature of a lifelong union between one man and one woman. Those whom God has joined together. And there are marriages that begin with God but which forget God and drift away from Him. Ask God to keep your marriage near to Him, in gratitude, in prayer, in communion with Him. God longs to share in it all with you. Be ready to share it all with Him.

Family life is one of God's own institutions, God's plan and pattern for our human race: father, mother, children. How often the family nowadays cannot be closely knit in all the ways it used to be. Difficulties about work, and travel to work, and getting a house, and many other difficulties besides. But with love and generosity and care for one another, the family, amid all these changes, can be a lovely thing still. Say a prayer for the family life of this country. Today all eyes will be on the Abbey, and the overwhelming reality at the heart of it all: beneath and beyond all the visible beauty, is God – God, the first reality of this day, God in the Abbey, God in your heart, God in your home, God in your marriage too. What a lot God gives us, and He wants us to give ourselves to Him.

Kate's Wedding

PETER WYLD

My niece Kate is getting married today and I've got to make a speech. They've allowed me anything from 35 to 45 seconds and God knows that's quite long enough for a speech from an old uncle – so aren't I lucky to have three or four whole minutes on the subject now. Irresistible to a bachelor.

One thing gives me a small pleasure. It's the thirteenth of the month and they're not being superstitious about it. I suppose silly superstitions don't really matter much, and one oughtn't to get in a fuss about them, but my goodness they can be strong. The one about thirteen I do find obnoxious because it's such a purely Christian superstition (you remember there were thirteen people who sat down at the Last Supper and one of them was Judas) . . . Oh dear, how bent and pointless the gospel can get on its way through our petty little minds. You know, I'm not at all sure I'd be happy myself to sit down thirteen to a meal. Isn't that pathetic? – so hurray for Kate and Christopher who've got that bit straight. Today is the convenient day for their wedding, so who cares that it's the thirteenth?

Kate's a bit special, the way nieces and nephews are apt to be. All that pleasure you get in the young for all those years, with none of the terrors of parenthood; and you don't have them there all the time either, the way parents and children have each other. I've got rows of nephews and nieces and they're all special and fantastically different; but Kate's my goddaughter and she was born on the day I got back from the war – England and spring and home and greenness and showing off – and this new baby with red hair. Lovely! So it's easy for me to be soppy about her.

So what do I wish her? Her and this nice man I hardly know, that she's marrying?

Kindness, I think.

Now don't get me wrong. I don't wish for them any kindness that's mushy or uncritical or cowardly or appeasing or lazy. Not any softy kindness at all. No conspiracy of mutual back-scratching to protect themselves from the world's weather in some snug, private world. No bargain struck to tell each other kind lies or shield each other from reality. That would be to exhaust each other's strength and humanity for the sake of safety. That would be to stop the outgoingness of love, to tell light not to shine. God save them from that sort of kindness to each other.

What I wish them is the kindness that starts from recognition, recognition of the staggering fact of their own *generosity*. Generosity on both sides that quite easily finds itself saying 'for better for worse'; generosity that you find just happens when you fall in love. The generosity I'm talking about puts (and it really does) the power over your own happiness plonk into another person's hands to see what they do with it. And what is needed, *demanded* in response, is kindness; kindness to meet and cherish the real and astonished vulnerability of loving and letting yourself be loved. The real nakedness. The real trust.

I think that sort of kindness, that trust, that generosity of the naked heart, is where maturity begins. It's the point at which, unprotected except by each other's kindness, you start to share and lose your private pride and your private fantasies and your private shames and your sulks and pomposities (which are all real enough, but still baby things for leaving behind). Then you start together, growing in the exchange of strength and tolerance, of irony and amusement, of affection and respect and acceptance. You start maturing to what St Paul calls 'the measure of the stature of the fullness of Christ' which I think means actually managing to grow, until you end up being really human. Being human *together*. Being human *like Jesus*. Being human in this way is an unending growth of maturity: man, naked and delighted and accepted by his Creator. This is what Christians believe men were created for nothing else but; and the theological name for it is Heaven.

That's where I think Kate and Christopher are going. And that's what I wish them.

Born Again

LEONARD BARNETT

For some years I lived in Epsom. And come Derby Day, I felt obliged to seek pastoral chances on the Downs. It's surprising how many parsons did the same. Also, on this occasion I have in mind, there was a patriarchal character witnessing to the truth as *he* saw it; he was holding aloft a text beloved of those who, bless their mistaken hearts, want to scare the rest of us nearer God.

THE END IS AT HAND! it said sombrely. I looked. The man was absolutely right. He was standing close by the finishing post.

He was right in every other way, too. The giant fact of life is that everything's on its way out – *and* getting renewed.

Take the outer man. Every month, we trade in the very skin that shapes us for a brand-new issue. It's the same inside. Most of our working parts aren't the same ones we set out with as we yelled our way into the world at birth. Nature's constantly doing an astounding repair and renewal job with heart, lungs, liver, blood and sinew. The end is always at hand; and a new start is always under way.

And what goes for our body, is good for our soul. I mean the essential you and me: sour or sunny, fussy or relaxed, openhanded, tightfisted, warm, cold . . . depending on whether or not we've yet dared to admit there's a renewal job waiting to be done. If we're honest, we won't need anyone to tell us. It's clear as day. Always has been; long before Christianity came in, too. Think of bald, paunchy little Socrates, a world of wisdom tucked inside that round head of his, praying daily like a little child, 'God, make me beautiful . . . inside'.

Think too of David, after the scandal with Bathsheba, praying, honest man that he was: 'Create in me a clean heart, O God, and renew a right spirit within me . . . blot out all mine iniquities . . .'

The fact is, said Jesus to Nicodemus, you've got to be born again. Born *again?* said Nicodemus, stalling. But of course, said Jesus. You must be born again into the kingdom of righteousness. And please shed the skin of *self*-righteousness as you pass through the waters of repentance into the world of the Spirit.

If any man is united to Christ, said Paul, he is a new creature. Such a one lives in a new world! It is a family world; and he displays the family spirit every day. Every day he hopes to get better at it; to be delivered from constantly blundering from bad to worse. He hopes that, changed from glory into glory, as Charles Wesley put it, even the incident called death isn't the end, but simply one more dramatic renewal; a translation, not a blotting-out.

Thank God for the fact of renewal! I almost want to lift up my voice and sing it – for the song's not over, and the melody isn't just lingering on. It's loud and clear; and every man's got a right to sing it.

Think of Christ's message: Return good for evil; give, don't grab; control your tongue so that it's kind, not cutting; do as you would be done by, not do unto others before they do it unto you. That's the new life for human beings which Jesus promised.

And no let-up, please. No getting writer's cramp before you've written a firm clear hand right down that new leaf you've turned over. The world's littered with self-made men who knocked off before they should. There's nothing very attractive about a half-made bed, a half-baked loaf, or a half-changed life. It's all or nothing.

We can never get away from ourselves, a psychologist once said. The whole problem of life is finding a self from which we never want to get away.

Jesus said: 'If anyone loses his life for my sake' – that is, if anyone lives for love and conquers self-love; champions truth and goodness and justice at whatever cost, come hell or high water – 'that man,' said Jesus, 'will find his true self'.

The Dark Days

H. J. RICHARDS

> Young man, remember God while you're still young,
> Remember him before the dark days come.

These words are from the last chapter of Ecclesiastes. The author has been searching again and again for the face of the hidden God. And here perhaps he's searching the hardest, as he reflects on old age, 'the dark days' as he calls them. The religious people of his time said that they were the brightest days, the sunset of life, the time when a man was closest to God. Isn't a ripe old age proof of a life well spent, God's reward for a life of virtue? Ecclesiastes has his doubts. Better serve the God you know while you're young, while you still have your wits about you.

I don't know any description of old age which surpasses the picture Ecclesiastes paints. He points to the indignity which old age brings to all a man's faculties, arms, back and legs, teeth, eyes and ears set in a head turning white like blossom on a tree:

> Don't wait until the sturdy guards are cowed,
> Until once straight-backed, mighty men are bowed,
> When all the grinders cease for they are few,
> And the eyes of window-peerers are wet with dew
> From a night out of which no new sun ever rose.
> Don't wait until some unseen hand shall close
> The door upon the bright and crowded street
> With its sounds of grinding and of scurrying feet.
> Don't wait until the twittering of a bird
> Can make you jump like sudden thunder heard.
> I tell the young, I tell them what I see!
> I see white blossom on the almond tree,
> Old grasshopper that drags himself along,
> Dead fires in dead hearts where they belong.

Only an old man could have written those lines, with their painful awareness of diminishing strength and failing faculties! 'I tell the young, I tell them what I see'. These indignities are what anyone can see in old people's homes, in psychiatric clinics, in the wards of terminal patients. Shall we put on rose-coloured spectacles when we describe the last phase of man's journey to his everlasting home? Or shall we simply tell what we see?

> Man there I see with mourners on the road;
> I see him going home to his abode
> Where he will live uncaring endlessly.
> My son, my son, these are the things I see.
> Soon, soon, the snapping of the silver thread,
> Soon breaks the golden lamp by which you've read;
> The pitcher at the fountain where it fell
> And soon the turning wheel beside the well.
> You too, and soon, like everything will break.
> The God who gives decidedly will take.
> Your dust you'll mix with dust within the grave,
> Your spirit render to the God who gave.
> Vanity of vanities! It seems to me
> No fool could doubt that all is vanity.

These are probably the most poignant lines in the whole of this remarkable book. Even the old age and the retirement to which so many people look forward to give them some respite from the rat race, even that only opens on to an emptiness darker than all the rest, when the silver thread snaps, and the golden lamp crashes, and the pitcher is smashed beyond repair. Ecclesiastes is not saying this with bitterness, but with infinite compassion and pity. Life is not as it's painted in the glossy brochures and the coloured magazines. There are aspects of it which can shatter anyone sensitive enough to look beneath the surface of things. Poor man, he says, poor man.

How did it happen, I wonder, that religious people ever accepted this book which questioned the meaning of life so disturbingly and so ruthlessly? Why didn't they condemn Ecclesiastes as a heretic for daring to criticise the answers people had given in the past to human misery? For, not only did they refuse to reject his writings; they treasured them as the work of a truly wise man. Why?

Perhaps because they saw that his questioning faith was more worthwhile than the faith which never asks questions. After all, who is the true believer, the man who simply repeats the answers his forefathers have handed on to him because they comfort him, or this 'disbeliever' who broke through to the realisation that we have to put our faith not in answers, but in God?

Confronting Old Age

FRANK HENNIG WITH FRED STREETER

Frank Hennig:
You can claim, Fred, the unusual distinction of having attended Sunday School from the age of four right up until you were fifteen.

Fred Streeter:
Yes, that's right, Frank, and you know, I learnt to say my prayers at my mother's knee. I was taught the way to go on and I tried to keep to that all my life, right up to the present day. Another thing, you must have faith, plenty of faith and you'll get through all right. We've got a tremendous lot to be thankful for and we never do thank God enough for what he has done for us. Just think, he produces everything, even the air which we breath. If he stopped that, well, we're done, ain't we?

Frank Hennig:
When you were a small boy living in a Sussex village, what was your idea of God?

Fred Streeter:
Well, I thought of him as an over-all Spirit and I still do. I think he's always with us. We can do nothing without him and, you know, we don't thank him very much, do we?

Frank Hennig:

Do you really feel that getting down on your knees and saying your prayers at night is something we should do as a natural part of every day?

Fred Streeter:

Oh yes. I'm fully convinced of that. I'm unable to kneel down now but I do say them in bed and I hope they'll be acceptable.

Frank Hennig:

When the time came for you to leave home, your mother – you were telling me – was very anxious you shouldn't lose touch with religion.

Fred Streeter:

That's right. She gave me the Bible and on the fly leaf was written, 'Fear God, Honour the King and Do unto others as you would that they would do to you'. Then, underneath, she wrote in her own hand, 'You follow this, my boy, and you won't go far wrong'. And, you know, I've had a glorious life really. All working amongst the flowers. I think of them just as I think of a lot of human beings.

Frank Hennig:

There is, of course, that old saying, 'You're nearer God's heart in a garden, than anywhere else on earth'. As a gardener, you believe that to be literally true, I suppose.

Fred Streeter:

Oh, yes! Never a truer word spoken, Frank. Every flower's got its life. And the more you think about it, the greater is the lesson.

Frank Hennig:

Some people might say, Fred, you've been fortunate as a gardener. You've led a fairly peaceful life, a life where you can feel you're pretty near to God. But how about the man working day by day in a factory? Or the man in a busy office? A little bit more difficult for them, perhaps, to appreciate what God means and what God can do.

Fred Streeter:
No, I shouldn't think so, not if they had a good training when they were young. Surely that still clings to them. After all, it doesn't take us very long – does it – not just to say a prayer night and morning?

Frank Hennig:
Would it be fair, Fred, to say that you're pretty conventional in your religion? You like traditional hymns. 'Love Divine All Loves Excelling' is your favourite, I think.

Fred Streeter:
Oh yes, I do. But I haven't got very much voice now, you know. I'm just an old gardener who likes to get out amongst the flowers still. But I haven't got the strength now.

Frank Hennig:
Is it true, do you think, that a sincere belief in God and Christianity is the sure way to happiness in its fullest sense?

Fred Streeter:
I'm absolutely certain it is. I never was surer of anything in my life. Keep your faith whatever you do.

Frank Hennig:
You say, 'Keep your faith no matter what' but there was a time in the First World War, for instance, when you were desperately seriously injured in battle. Didn't your faith begin to waver for a moment or two then?

Fred Streeter:
No, Frank. When I was in the trenches, I prayed that I might be restored back to my old life, which was what happened. And on the stretcher one of these little flower girls put a bunch of chrysanths on the stretcher and she said, 'Are you all right? You're back in England now'. I thought she was an angel. I didn't think I was on earth at all.

Frank Hennig:
Many people are firmly convinced that you, Fred Streeter, are indestructible but, like all of us, one of these days, you're going to die. What's your particular approach to the thought of death? Does it worry you?
Fred Streeter:
No, not a bit, Frank. I've had a good life. I've tried to be prepared to go whenever my time comes; and I'm looking forward to eternity.
Frank Hennig:
What are your thoughts about heaven? What'll happen to you when you die?
Fred Streeter:
If I can still keep my old job, Frank . . . When I get to the Gates of Heaven and meet St Peter, the Gate Keeper, I shall ask, 'Is there any chance of me coming in?' And he says, 'What have you been in life?' 'Oh,' I says, 'well . . . I've *tried to be* a gardener.' 'Oh,' he says, 'come in, come in, come in, we've got plenty of weeds in here wants killing.'
Frank Hennig:
So Fred Streeter will very quickly have his coat off in Heaven.
Fred Streeter:
Yes, I will. And God bless you all.

Comfort in Bereavement

C. A. JOYCE

Some time ago I was asked to speak at a Remembrance Service held at a crematorium. Sitting on the lawns in an amphitheatre surrounded by lovely trees and gardens there were over 5000 people. There were Roman Catholics, Methodists, Church of England – and some who professed no religion at all. For example, one man said to me: 'Thank you for a lovely service. I don't believe in any religion myself, but I come here once a year especially to remember my brother.' I think he may be nearer the Kingdom than he knows.

All those people were gathered, and for once united, in remembrance. It is interesting how death makes possible a unity that life hasn't yet succeeded in bringing about.

Throughout my life many people have said to me: 'Mr Joyce, I have suffered, and am still suffering, the grievous loss of someone I loved. Will you say something about that – if there is anything to say?' Perhaps I may be permitted to *try* at any rate.

First of all, I want to ask a question: Are we quite sure that our grief and our sorrow isn't in some measure self-pity? After all, we can't be sorry for *them*, can we? The Bible tells us why: 'They shall hunger no more, neither thirst any more; and God shall wipe away all tears from their eyes'.

Our tears remain because of the loneliness, the hurt, the grief we have to endure. God knows that this is very natural and that in it there is nothing wrong or feeble. But I would like you to join me for a moment in some very practical thinking. Imagine that *you* had died instead, and left your partner to carry on alone as you are doing. The loneliness and the heartbreak would be theirs, not yours, and all your suffering would be theirs alone. Would you really wish that for them? Of course not, so you go on bearing your pain for them, making what is called vicarious sacrifice on their behalf. May God strengthen you as you carry that burden. As we grow older we can say with the poet, Lawrence Binyon:

> They shall not grow old as we that are left grow old:
> Age shall not weary them, nor the years condemn . . .

One of the most painful things we have to endure when someone we love dies is *our own remorse*. In his *Confessions*, St

Augustine, who wasn't a very good son to his mother when she was alive, describes her death and his remorse:

> At Ostia, where the Tiber runs into the sea, I watched my mother die. I was the one who smudged her eyelids into place. She died happy; but she had not always been so. I was, I must confess, the main source of her sorrow.
>
> When I closed her eyes, a sea of sorrow surged across my heart and tears flooded my eyes. I repressed them. I silenced the urgent cry, like that of sea-birds, in my heart. Never to see her again or hear her sweet voice.

How many of the bereaved have similar pangs of conscience. I have met scores of people who say regretfully, 'Oh! I wish I had done more for them when they were alive! I keep reproaching myself for the things I could have done and didn't do'. I think that is absolutely wrong and that it is hurting the people we have 'loved and lost awhile'. You see, I believe that they have memories, too, but they are full of happiness because they are full of understanding now. They have got things in their right perspective. How do I justify that? Because the Bible tells me so: 'Now we see through a glass darkly, but then face to face. Now we know in part . . . but then I shall know even as I am known'.

Putting it practically and very simply, I don't think that my mother spends her time remembering what I *didn't* do, but rather what we did do happily together.

Finally, what about funerals and graves and so on? I would just like to say that a coffin doesn't contain the person I loved and still love. It is where that person used to live. I don't remember my mother any better by going and standing outside the house where she lived a long time ago. I think we go to a funeral not just as a mark of respect for the memory of one we loved so well, but even more, I hope, to share and sympathise with those who remain and who need our love and our sympathy more than ever now in their sorrow and loss.

Sometimes I wish that we could talk more often and more freely about those who are not with us in this life any more, and not behave as if they were no longer part of our being and our life. 'Gone', certainly, but not for ever, and certainly not 'forgotten'. By talking of them, they continue as part of life.

In a book called *A Warrior on Wings* the Reverend A. Price-Hughes wrote:

> If I should die and leave you here awhile,
> Be not like others sore undone who keep
> Lone vigils by the silent dust and weep:
> For my sake, turn again to life and smile,
> Nerving thy heart and trembling hand to do
> Something to comfort weaker hearts than thine.
> Complete these dear unfinished tasks of mine,
> And I, perchance, may therein comfort you.

It seems to me that in this way we turn our sacrifice of sorrow into service.

Ten Commandments for the Brassed-Off Citizen

COLIN MORRIS

Loitering around a petrol pump the other day, I whiled away the time composing Ten Commandments for the brassed-off citizen. I doubt if they'll earn me immortality, but they might start a train of thought – which could be the only train running!

One:

Let's not waste time looking for scapegoats to blame our

present plight on, whether they be strikers, politicians, oil sheikhs or garage attendants. Better by far to identify that bit of the crisis we ourselves have helped to create by our selfishness or apathy. Deal with *them* and we might become part of the answer rather than the problem.

Two:

When we shudder at our present predicament, let's spare a thought for that large part of the world's population who would dearly love to be in it. They're scratching around not for the odd gallon of petrol to fuel their car but for the odd crust to feed their kids.

Three:

Beware of any leader, politician, industrialist, financier or trade unionist who lacks a sense of humour in a time of crisis. He has no defence against self-idolatory, and there are enough false gods inviting our worship at the moment without adding to their number.

Four:

Talking of false gods, we've made a god out of growth only to find he has feet of sand. Now's the time to replace *Bigger* and *Better* as the basis of our values. Excellence is the only worthwhile goal of any human activity.

Five:

When you hear astronomic figures bandied about by economists and others, remember that *other* statistic which shows that Man is the costliest investment of all time. It took four billion years of evolutionary pain to produce him. Hence, the poorest man is infinitely more valuable than the most expensive commodity.

Six:

We didn't come *into* this world, we came *out* of it. If God is our Father, Earth is our Mother, but if we don't stop pillaging, poisoning and polluting her, then generations yet unborn won't be.

Seven:
As Confucius never said: Better no transport than no legs. Don't let pathos or indignation at our plight blind us to those in our own society who are robbed of their basic human entitlement: a sound mind in a whole body, and enough food and shelter to keep both together. They have absolute priority in the queue for what's going.
Eight:
Whenever men try to corner the market in scarce commodities, they are returning a negative answer to that old Biblical question, 'Am *I* my brother's keeper?' My brother doesn't need a keeper; he needs a brother.
Nine:
Some of my best friends, as the saying goes, are advertising experts, but I hope they'll forgive me for pointing out that if it costs tens of thousands of pounds to persuade me I need something, then I don't.
Ten:
When the world's in a mess – and when wasn't it? – Someone up there is telling us something. I think I hear him saying, you *can* survive, with limited supplies of physical energy, provided you make up the shortfall with an irreplaceable commodity: compassion. Turn *that* tap off and the most affluent society will become as cold and lifeless as a polar ice-cap. For what's the point of having everything if no one cares whether you live or die?

God cares, which means *we* ought to. So back to the drawing board to design a society which elevates real quality above endless quantity.

Freedom and Permissiveness

BISHOP TREVOR HUDDLESTON

No one in this country today would dare suggest that we have achieved a perfect social order. Certainly not those who govern us, for they have been saying very clearly that inflation, for example, is the symptom of a sick society. Certainly not those who oppose the government, for they have been saying that massive unemployment and job-insecurity are symptoms of a sick society, too. So it is not presumptuous, nor does it mean that we are 'knocking Britain', if we try as Christians to see what is defective, what needs remedial treatment in our country today.

I think that one of our greatest difficulties in Britain today is that we have allowed a mood of introspectiveness to take hold of us. We've been concerned for so long about our condition, balance of payments, cost of living, inflation, growth-rate and the like that we have become neurotic. The only thing we can think about is our economic temperature, and we put the thermometer under our tongue every ten minutes to make sure we are still alive!

In my view, it is quite certainly the duty of the Church not simply to minister to the needs, both spiritual and material, of man where he is, but to exercise its prophetic role as well. It is too easily forgotten that the Christ who said, 'Come unto me all ye who labour and are heavy-laden and I will give you rest', said also, 'I am not come to bring peace but a sword'. What he meant, surely, was that a Christian voice, faithfully proclaiming the word of God, is as often divisive, provocative, stern, as it is reconciling, healing and compassionate.

What, then, as a Christian, do I see to be wrong with our society in Britain today?

Many people ascribe all our ills to one cause: they say that society is far too permissive. By permissiveness they mean a widespread breakdown of moral standards, particularly those which affect or control family life. They instance sexual promiscuity; the increase in pornography of every kind; the indiscipline of students; the rise in crimes of violence, mugging and the like; the drug-scene; the abortion rate and so on. They might also use the kind of language which Malcolm Muggeridge delights in, and uses so effectively, to castigate both the permissive society itself and those (like the 'trendy bishops' of the Church of England) who appear to condone it. In the first volume of his autobiography, he writes:

> It has long seemed abundantly clear to me that I was born into a dying, if not already dead, civilisation . . . echoing with the hyena cries of Freudians looking for their Marx and Marxists looking for their Freud . . . From St Augustine to St Ezra Pound, from Plainsong to the Rolling Stones, from El Greco to Picasso, from Chartres to the Empire State Building, from Benvenuto Cellini to Henry Miller, from Pascal's *Pensées* to Robinson's *Honest to God.* A Gadarene descent down which we all must slide, finishing up in the same slough.[1]

[1]Malcolm Muggeridge, *Chronicles of Wasted Time*, Collins, 1972, p.15.

It is not difficult to attribute the ills of our society to permissiveness defined in this sort of way. On the contrary, it is far too easy.

What is basically wrong with our society, as I see it, is not the kind of freedom we call permissiveness, but the kind of permissiveness we call freedom. We have in fact lost the true meaning of freedom and we need most urgently to discover why.

We are so conditioned in these days to an acceptance of the opinions of sociologists, scientists, psychologists and the like that we are in danger of forgetting that Christianity itself has something to say to people about freedom. In a sense, freedom is what the Gospel is all about. St Paul in Romans 8 says that the universe itself is to be *freed* from the shackles of mortality and enter upon the *liberty* and splendour of the children of God. What, then, is the nature of this liberty?

St Augustine draws a distinction, which I find helpful, between what he calls 'liberty' – the perfect freedom of God's children which men are *meant* to have, the freedom which enables men to be truly free, to be themselves – and 'free-will' – which is the freedom men in fact *do* have.

The protagonists of the permissive society are claiming above all else that men should be *free to be themselves*. In response Christianity says that this is the case already: men *have* free-will, and always have had it. But that *as they are* they are not free to be free.

Men are not free to be free unless they grasp two mysterious but fundamental facts concerning their nature. The first is that man is capable of relationship not only with his fellow-men, but also with God. He is in fact made for God. In Augustine's words, he is restless till he rests in God.

The second is what we call the problem of evil, 'the fact', as someone has said, 'that the human situation *itself* (not just contemporary society in Britain or Europe) is characterised by a twist or flaw'. In the traditional language of the Church, this means that man lives in a fallen world.

When we look at the ills of our social order and ascribe them all to permissiveness, we should remember that the cure for permissiveness is freedom: it is 'the glorious liberty of the children of God' who know that they *are* his children and who know, too, that all human structures and institutions are marred and, in some way, spoiled.

The Binmen of Belfast

ROBIN WILLIAMSON

Are not two sparrows sold for a penny? And not one of them will fall to the ground without your Father's will. But even the very hairs of your head are all numbered. (Matthew 10: 29, 30.)

Not so long ago the binmen of Belfast had a strike. In press, radio and television many people spoke bitterly against their strike. People whose memories are short said harsh things about the binmen.

I wonder how many people remember the morning of 20 March 1972. It rained that morning but the sun peeped through the cloudy skies. A Corporation garbage collection vehicle crept out of a side street in the Belfast city centre, one of the fleet which is the pride of the Corporation Cleansing Department. The light grey tank-like vehicle was proof of the normality of life within the heart of our city.

The rain slowly stopped and the streets began to dry. The great grey vehicle moved slowly down the damp street. The Corporation dust-cart was late, almost half an hour late. But the weather was bad and her crew didn't want to get soaked so early in the day. Better late than soaked to the skin for the rest of the working day.

The men who formed the crew of the dust-cart were a bit impatient. They wanted to stop for a quiet smoke somewhere dry, they wanted a chat and a cup of tea in that homely vehicle cab. There were the dogs to pick at Dunmore Park and the horses running on the English tracks. But the dust-cart just lazed along, crawling a few inches from the kerb, as they went from house to house and shop to shop on their city centre round.

There was plenty of time for the six-man crew of that Corporation cart to do their work and to think of their cup of tea. The six-man crew were all regulars. Friends of many trips. The clouds began to break up over Belfast, and time crept on. The binmen talked among themselves and joked with passers-by.

The Corporation cart made its way along the street. Past the morning newspaper offices. Every few feet picking up the waste of an affluent society. The driver pulled away from the kerb and looked in his mirror as he passed a badly parked van. Then back along the kerb again. The driver raised the back of his truck to bring the rubbish forward, and the children loved it.

The time in that narrow Belfast Street was three minutes to twelve on Monday 20 March 1972. From somewhere in a badly parked van behind the dust-cart a tiny spark jumped. A spark so small that the naked eye couldn't have seen it. And in less time than it takes to tell, the parked van exploded.

Flames leapt from her metal bodywork, flames of red, yellow and lilac wrapped in deep grey smoke. From the Belfast Corporation dust-cart the bodies flew. People screamed. Pieces of human flesh littered the street. Some lay for ever still while others incredibly picked themselves up and staggered shocked away.

Six people died in that instant of time in Donegal Street, Belfast, on Monday 20 March 1972 at 11.57 a.m. Protestant and Roman Catholic they died together as they have so often since in other outrages. Old and young: they all died together. How many names can *you* remember?

> Comfort ye, comfort ye my people . . .
> Not one of them will fall to the ground without
> your Father's will.

Good out of Evil

ERIC JAMES

There's a magic for most of us about islands: the Isle of Wight, the Channel Islands, the Hebrides.

Not long ago, I had the enormous privilege of spending six weeks in the Solomon Islands in the South Pacific, just over a thousand miles from the north-east coast of Australia. I'm one of the agents in England for the Bishop of the Solomons, the Bishop of Melanesia, as he's called, and I was having a look at the work of the Church there.

Because of its part in the Second World War, almost everyone will have heard of the main island, Guadalcanal. I don't think any piece of territory illustrates more graphically for me the mystery of good and evil in this world.

I was staying in the Bishop's house on Guadalcanal for three weeks. It's not more than fifty yards from the sea-shore – a wonderful coral coast-line that looks out over blue-green waters to distant grey islands. What clouds there are, are most often white puffs in clear blue sky.

But the sea you look out on has terrible wartime memories. Indeed, in front of the Bishop's house, half in the sea and half on the coral beach, lies, vivid green, the rusted seaweeded remains of an American transport of thirty years ago.

As I sat on the veranda of the Bishop's house in the early hours of the morning, my mind would often go back to those years. It was in March 1942 that Japanese raids began on one of the grey islands which I could see in the distance, and these were repeated until the Japanese landed on the main island itself.

In July 1942 the Japanese started work on an airfield on Guadalcanal. That airfield today is the International Airport for the Solomons. The building of that wartime airfield is in fact directly responsible for the bringing of so many of the gifts of civilisation to the Solomons: all that is indispensable for the development of a country, medicine, education, industry, technology.

You can walk along the coast road between that airfield and Honiara, the capital of the Solomons, seven miles to the east of the airfield, and then on another couple of miles to the west of Honiara to the Bishop's house. On the way, you pass many notices marking the terrible battles for that road. If the earth beneath the shops and offices of Honiara, beneath the new Cathedral and the new Government buildings, could tell its own tale, every inch of it would be a tale of death in war.

And yet that coast road, built by the Americans, is now literally a life-line making possible the development, for instance, of midwifery and other forms of social medicine all along the coast. That road has led to the clearance of most of the island from malaria. At one place along that road there is still the remains of half a Liberator lying in a field, and not far beyond, a vast pile of rusting ironwork on the beach, the heaped-up remains of Japanese and American warships.

When you stand in the little port of Honiara and look out to sea, you look across what is now called Iron Bottom Sound, because in that narrow stretch of water so many ships were sunk. Japanese: two battleships, three destroyers, nine transports. American: one battleship, two anti-aircraft cruisers, eight destroyers. All this from only one of the battles fought there. But the port which was created in the war is now a vital part of the development not only of Guadalcanal but of all the Solomon islands. Perhaps you will understand what I mean by this territory illustrating so graphically the mystery of good and evil.

I don't personally find it surprising that good and evil are so mysteriously intertwined, indeed that often good rises from the ashes of some situation of terrible evil.

We all speak so naturally, for instance, of *Good* Friday. But the story of Jesus is above all the story of wickedness and cruelty, betrayal of the innocent and injustice. It's the story of *Bad* Friday. Only Jesus' love, courage and self-sacrifice turned it into Good Friday.

I found myself seeing Guadalcanal in the light of the Cross. All the works of education, and medicine and civilisation now taking place there on that wartime site were a sign of hope: a sign that in any situation – whether in the South Pacific or here at home – evil need never have the last word. The last word is with good, the good which the Christian believes was most clearly revealed in Christ on his cross.

The Birth of Christ

H. J. RICHARDS

As you come into this little town of Bethlehem, you're greeted by a large banner across the road which reads, in Hebrew, 'Beruchim Habaim – Blessed is he who comes'; and underneath it, in Arabic, 'Ahlan veSahalan – My tent is yours'. It's a great joy to be welcomed so gracefully to one's ancestral home. Because coming to Bethlehem as a Christian, you have the feeling of going back to your roots.

The great basilica of the Nativity, as it is called, stands in the centre of the town. It was built more than 1600 years ago over the cave which the early Christians venerated as the place where Jesus was born. The roofing that you see above you as you go in is, they say, English oak, donated by King Edward III at a time the church was in need of restoration. The Crusaders who rescued the church from the Saracens walled up the doors to stop soldiers riding in on horseback, and for centuries the only entrance to the vast interior has been a tiny little postern gate, where you have to bend almost double to avoid banging your head.

At the far end of the church some steps cut into the rock go down into the cave, and here too you have to stoop quite low until you stand in the cave, as I'm doing now, looking at the silver star set into the ground and the inscription, 'Here, of the Virgin Mary, was born Jesus Christ'.

It's a sort of parable, I've always thought, when I've visited Bethlehem, that no one can come and see the place where Jesus was born without making this act of humility and obeisance. It's as if the very stones are saying to you, 'You've got to stoop here, pilgrim, this place where God has stooped so low for you'.

It is, indeed, a very strange thing that we have to preach to the world, those of us who believe in Christ: that God is no longer to be looked for where people do tend to look for him, up there, out yonder, up in the heavens. He is only here, in something as utterly human as the birth of a child. 'But that doesn't *look* like God', we can hear ourselves saying, and the reply comes back, 'Who knows what God looks like?' 'Well, this is nothing like *my* idea of God', we say, and the reply is, 'Very likely; it's your idea of God which has to go'.

The birth of Christ, for those who believe in him, means that from this moment on, the indescribable mystery which we call God can only be found in someone entirely like you and me. What the Christian is really trying to say at Christmas is, 'I believe in Man'.

The first people who heard this strange teaching called it atheism. 'This,' they said, 'is emptying the heavens and getting rid of the gods. Away with these godless people.' It could be that those first persecutions have given us Christians a sort of subconscious phobia, so that we've been scared ever since to say openly what our origins here at Bethlehem proclaim: we believe in Man.

The Peace of Christ

MICHAEL STANCLIFFE

Man is the noisiest of all animals. With his voice, his implements, his machines and all the equipment of sound transmission and amplification, he has created the great rackety din and pandemonium which is the inescapable background against which so many have to try to work and live. Some seem to enjoy noise – enjoy making it, anyhow – just as there are some who believe that noise, like speed, is a symbol of virility and power. And of course it is – of an animal or mechanical kind. But pandemonium means literally 'totally devilish'. It is the noise of Hell. It weakens, disintegrates and finally destroys what is human. It is one of the greatest enemies of our physical and mental health, and a major source of the pollution of our environment.

In view of this, it is worth reflecting on the peace and silence of Jesus. We don't pay enough attention these days to the size of the part played by silence in his life: you know, those thirty years of silence before ever he began to preach and teach; the way he repeatedly took himself off and away from people and into the stillness of lonely places; the astonishing silence he maintained virtually throughout the long hours of his trial and execution.

One of the most telling characteristics of Jesus was his stillness. In him the busy, the dizzy and the demented found peace and calm and new health. Lunatics were found sitting calmly at his feet, clothed and in their right minds. 'Come unto me, all ye that travail and are heavy laden, and I will refresh you.' That was his invitation. So Mary came and sat at his feet and was still, and busy Martha was told to stop fussing and doing things and to follow her sister's example. Incidentally, the fact that so many of us feel that Martha was rather unfairly rebuked indicates how deeply we recognise that the rebuke applies to us.

When words were needed, those that Jesus spoke were short and to the point – no clever chat to get a string of cheap laughs, no idle gossip, no noisy boasting. Such words as he spoke were recognised as words of love, of truth, and of no ordinary power and authority, as this gospel story shows:

> On that day, when evening had come, he said to them, 'Let us go across to the other side'. And leaving the crowd, they took him with them in the boat, just as he was. And other boats were with him. And a great storm of wind arose, and the waves beat into the boat, so that the boat was already filling. But he was in the stern, asleep on the cushion; and they woke him and said to him, 'Teacher, do you not care if we perish?' And he awoke and rebuked the wind, and said to the sea, 'Peace! Be still!' And the wind ceased, and there was a great calm. He said to them, 'Why are you afraid? Have you no faith?' And they were filled with awe, and said to one another, 'Who then is this, that even wind and sea obey him?' (Mark 4: 35–41.)

Experienced boatmen panicked around him, even accused him of having no concern for them – but Jesus had only to say to the elements, 'Hush. Be still', and there was a great calm.

Even when the wildest storm of human sin and demonic evil broke and crashed upon him his stillness remained. Cross-examined by men hell-bent on his destruction, he held his peace. 'He held his peace' is the old Authorised Version phrase, and wonderfully telling it is. In spite of all that was being done to him he had peace – and he *held* it. Nailed to the cross he remained unmoved while noisy men made rings round him and taunted him to prove his divinity – which he did, by staying where he was and holding on to his peace. Weakness? On the contrary. Far from being mastered by his enemies, he mastered them, as the judgement of history has recognised. Such stillness and silence generate power, immense power, power radiating a pardon and peace that we still know.

From the stillness and silence of Jesus' tomb resurrection came. Judas, so dizzy with his twistings that he could not keep still, went and hanged himself. But those others who had been closest to Jesus came together again after the first panic; with much fear, if not much faith, they waited and kept still and quiet. This is how they came to know the risen Christ, to be given his peace, to be filled with his power.

The Parables of Christ

KENNETH SIMS

One of my favourite toys when I was a small boy was a thing called a 'Snake Camera'. A perfectly innocent-looking camera, it was, and I used to point it at people and invite them to stand quite still while I took their photo. But, of course, you know what happened next. Inside the camera was a rubber snake curled up on a spring, and the moment you pressed the button, it would spring out hitting the innocent victim on the nose.

I was reminded of this toy the other day when I came across something P. G. Wodehouse once said about the Parables of Christ. 'A parable,' said Wodehouse, 'is one of those jolly Bible stories which starts off as a pleasant yarn, but which keeps something up its sleeve which suddenly jumps out and knocks you flat.'

Not a bad definition of a parable. Those picturesque stories about the Sower and the Good Samaritan and the Prodigal Son, which we all learned in our Sunday School days, always contained some point, some unexpected challenge, which gave people something to think about.

Take the story of the man who was ploughing a field when, suddenly, the plough jarred to a stop and a sharp metallic sound rang out as the coulter struck something hard. It proved to be an old chest full of coins and precious stones.

Now, when Christ first told this story in Galilee, at this point the crowd must have been all ears, listening eagerly. Story-tellers were very popular in Palestine, and there was nothing people liked more than a story of Hidden Treasure. No doubt, from time to time, this sort of thing did actually happen. For centuries, men had known what it was to have to pack up suddenly in the middle of the night and leave their farms and homesteads because of the threatened invasion of some army on the march; and quite often a man would hastily bury his life's savings in the ground, hoping one day to come back and recover his wealth. And, quite often, he never returned; and so it was not an uncommon thing for someone to stumble upon an unexpected hidden treasure. Of course, everyone must have dreamed of doing this, just as people dream of winning the Football Pools today. Someone had to be the lucky one, and news of a 'find' always caused a sensation and raised everyone's hopes.

So the people listening to Jesus would have loved this story. 'Go on then!' they would cry, 'tell us what happened next!'

'Ah,' said the Story-teller – and this is where the snake began to pop out of the camera – 'you know what happened next. This man ploughing the field had to buy it in order to claim the hidden treasure. That's the law isn't it?' They all nodded in agreement, because that *was* the law in those days. 'And so,' Jesus went on, 'because the price of the field was pretty high, the man had to sell everything he possessed in order to raise enough cash. But it was worth it, he couldn't afford to be without that treasure.'

The people listening to this parable got the point all right. They knew that this was a story about the Kingdom of God. As they listened, while they were seeing in their imagination the farmer going about the market place and selling everything he had, they were really thinking of all the things that they themselves would have to surrender before they could possess the treasure that Christ had come to offer them. And what a treasure it was – a faith that nothing could destroy, a hope that would shine through every dark surrounding cloud, a love that would never let them go.

So, some of them gave up their false gods of materialism and selfishness and self-choosing, so that they could have instead these treasures of God which could strengthen them in heart and spirit, and transform life into something really worth living.

In his parables, Christ is still speaking to us today. If we listen carefully to them, we, too, will discover the things that *none of us* can afford to be without.

The Miracles of Christ

WILLIAM BARCLAY

How can Christ's miracles mean anything to us in the twentieth century? To answer this we are going to look at the story of the turning of the water into wine in the second chapter of John's Gospel.

You remember the story. Jesus was at a wedding party in the village of Cana in Galilee. Some of his disciples were with him and Mary his mother was there too. And during the party a disaster happened – the wine began to go done. If the wine finally did go done, that would be a shame that the young couple would never be able to forget. In a Jewish house hospitality was everything, and people would never have forgotten the party at which the wine went done.

So Mary came to Jesus and she told him about it. And Jesus said to her: 'Look, mother. Just you leave this to me. When the time comes I'll act all right.' There were six great stone jars there. The water in them was not for drinking; it was for cleansing the hands and the feet after the walk with open sandals on the dusty roads. They were vast jars holding each of them between twenty and thirty gallons. Jesus said to the servants: 'Fill the jars, right up – to the very brim.' They did so. 'Now,' he said, 'draw some of the water out of the jars and take it to the master of ceremonies and offer it to him to drink.' So they did. And when the master of ceremonies tasted it, his face lit up. 'Most people,' he said, 'lay on the best wine first, and then when people have had quite a good bit to drink, then they lay on the inferior wine, hoping that by that time no one will notice it. But you,' he said, 'you have kept the best wine till now.'

What about this story? If all it means is that at a wedding party Jesus manufactured some wine, has it really got anything to say to us at all? Suppose Jesus did turn jars of water into wine, so what?

Well, then, if you read John's miracle stories carefully, you will see John flashing you a red light to warn you that there is more in this than meets the eye. Look back at the story. There were six stone jars; they held twenty to thirty gallons of water each. If Jesus turned that water into wine, he provided the party with something between 120 and 180 gallons of wine – an awful lot of wine – getting on for a thousand bottles of wine. Some party!

So John says, 'Stop a minute! Think!' It's not really possible to think that this is meant to be taken literally. Now think again. I believe that the great danger is to think of Jesus as a person who *did* wonderful things, instead of a person who *does:* and that the real meaning of it is that when

Jesus comes into life it is like water turning into wine.

Grenfell was the great Labrador doctor. He often tried to get people to come and help him to heal people in the frozen north. He wrote to one of the nurses in the great John Hopkins hospital: 'If you want to have the time of your life, come with me and run a hospital next summer for the orphans of the Northland. There will not be a cent of money in it for you, and you will have to pay your own expenses. But I'll guarantee that you will feel a love for life you have never before experienced. It's having the time of anyone's life to be in Christ's service.'

I'm quite sure that this is what this story about Jesus means. The point of it is not that he turned water into wine for a wedding party nineteen hundred and fifty years ago. The point is that *now*, *today* he can make life sparkle and scintillate just as if flat water was turned into thrilling wine.

There's a verse of a hymn that sums it up:

Heaven above is softer blue,
  Earth around is sweeter green;
Something lives in every hue,
  Christless eyes have never seen:
Birds with gladder songs o'erflow,
  Flowers with deeper beauties shine,
Since I know, as now I know,
  I am his, and he is mine.

Suffering with Christ

RALPH ROLLS WITH MOTHER TERESA

I met Mother Teresa in London recently. She'd just come from Belfast on a brief visit before going on to France and then to Italy. I was surprised to learn how widespread her work had become in recent years. It seemed that wherever there was disaster or poverty or strife or sickness or despair, Mother Teresa had been there, opened a house or a hostel or a camp or a centre – so that she and the brothers and sisters of her order could set about serving the people in the name of Christ.

They're serving in Amman, Bangladesh, Belfast, Melbourne, Venezuela – and in London too. Here are her words:

> I think the people in England do not know their poor, and because they don't know them, it's very difficult to love them, and still more difficult to serve them. If you could only bring the people face to face. For example, a Sister is trying to get a shelter, a home where we can bring in these people who are dying of cold outside, so old and so unwanted and so unloved and so lonely. I think this is the greatest poverty that a human being has to go through.

I put it to Mother Teresa that many would be surprised to know that there are such people still uncared for in London. She replied:

> I think they know in figures but they don't know face to face. There *are* people who are sleeping in the streets of London, and there *are* people who have to use cardboard for sleeping on, and there *are* people who are shivering and nearly half-frozen in the midst of London. Others have no time, they have no time for people like that. And this not having time is the greatest suffering for our poor people. They are not wanted. Also there is another kind of suffering here, the loneliness of our old people living by themselves in one little room. Even the next-door neighbour doesn't know their name and never thinks of giving them a glass of water. This is the greatest, greatest disease in the world today.

Yet strangely enough the saints seem to be able to see something positive, even creative, in suffering. And they don't avoid the issue by just saying it's a mystery either. Mysteries are singularly unconsoling to one who has to suffer. No, the Christian saints see something positive in it. Mother Teresa is no exception. For her, suffering is a gift.

> Suffering by itself is nothing; it's useless. But suffering shared with Christ in his passion is a wonderful gift to human life. It is the most beautiful gift for us to share in the passion of Christ, yes, and a sign of love, because His Father proved that He loved the world by giving His Son to die for us, and so in Christ's own life it was proved that suffering was the gift, the greatest gift. As our Lord has said, 'Greater love than this no man has that he gives his life for his friends'. And so when we suffer for Jesus, this is the greatest love, the undivided love.

I suggested that to say suffering is a gift is a hard message to those who are afflicted. A hard message, she said, but true. I asked her if she could give me an instance of someone who had been able to see suffering as a gift through realising that he was sharing in the Passion of Christ. So she told me this story of a man in Calcutta who'd been brought to her home for the dying.

> The Sister in charge explained to him the Passion of Christ. He had a terrible headache, and so she told him how Jesus bore the crown of thorns. Different parts of the Passion she explained to him, and this had a certain effect on his life. He refused morphine after that; he wanted to share in that passion.
>
> When I went back one day to the hospital, I saw death on his face, and I said to him: 'I'm so glad that your suffering will be finished and you won't have to suffer any more of this pain and this torture'. He looked at me and

said, 'I do not want to die. I want to share with him who loved me first'. And then, 'My God, I love you,' and he died.

The Death and Resurrection of Christ

GEOFFREY LAMPE

'There is a green hill far away . . . Where the dear Lord was crucified, Who died to save us all.' The simple words of the old hymn make an astonishing and far from simple claim. They say that the death of Jesus of Nazareth in a distant city many hundreds of years ago can save us now.

'Save us': that means, set us free from the self-centred lovelessness that cuts us off from God and from our brother men.

Why the *death* of Jesus? Why is the cross always the sign that stands for Jesus and for Christian faith? Because his death is the moment that focuses his whole life. It is the key to his life. It's the perfect summing-up of all that he was. It's the great climax of all that he did.

St Paul said, 'We shall be saved by Jesus' life'. That is because in that life of Jesus the basic sinfulness of man was annulled. In our lives, self-satisfaction, complacent pride, defensive anxiety, are constantly cutting us off from love and denying us the freedom to be loving people. But in Jesus all this had no place at all. He was fully open to God's love, free to love other people genuinely and spontaneously, even though they might be quite unlovable. He loved the outcasts of his society, the tax-officials, the women of the streets like Magdalen.

Not that all this was easy for him. He was strongly tempted to go the way of the rest of us: to put self-preservation first, to chase popularity, to get his hands on the levers of power.

But he never lost his trust in God. He never failed in his determination to do God's will. It was doing God's will that brought him to his death. His total response to God's love actually brought him to the breaking-point of trust: the dreadful sense that in the end God had deserted him. 'My God, my God, why have you forsaken me?' But never was Jesus closer to God than in the moment of despair. In Jesus' death, his life of trust and obedience reached its splendid climax. On the cross we see the triumph of divine love, and we see a new possibility for human life: life where sin has been taken out of the way, because selfishness has been changed into self-giving.

Wonderful for Jesus: if a two-thousand-year-old story is *really* true. But even if this one man did live a perfect life, does that make any difference to us now? If Jesus were only a character in the book, it wouldn't. We might admire him, and we might try to copy him. But we in the twentieth century can't really imitate the life-style of a first-century peasant in Palestine. Nor have we got the power to change ourselves into people like him. We need him to love *us* with his divine love: not just the people he met long ago.

But so he does. That's why his death can save us all. He isn't just a character in a book. He's alive. Here and now the living Spirit of Jesus grips people and brings them love and joy and hope. I believe that in this sense Jesus has met me and touched my life.

The Church of Christ

THE ARCHBISHOP OF CANTERBURY

The Church of Christ stands for something very different from what society as a whole in any country stands for. It says to its own members and to all who will listen, 'Here is the true way of life taught by Christ and seen in Christ'. Inevitably this bears upon issues of a social and political kind. The Church for instance has to say that racial discrimination is always wrong, that it is a duty to care about people in poverty and hunger, that life-long marriage is a sacred institution – to give a few instances. And the more consistent the Church is, the more it may have clashes with a good deal of popular opinion.

So the Church is pledged to influence society and to criticise society. In this, its deepest influence should always be upon persons in their character as persons. Christ himself lived and died and rose again in a world full of social abuses, including the appalling abuse of slavery. But his chief method was not to attack institutions but to transform people. And there can be no substitute for the impact of Christianity upon people at the deepest level. But a person never lives in a vacuum; he is always a bundle of social relationships both private and public, and these all need to become Christianised. You might be a most sincerely good and devout person and yet fail to see that some of your attitudes about persons or about society were far from the teaching of Jesus Christ. When Jesus denounced the Pharisees for hypocrisy, he didn't mean insincerity or pretence: he meant rather the way very sincere people can wear blinkers about some of their attitudes and actions.

So the Church's mission to change personal lives cannot be separated from its critique of wrong attitudes in society. It must answer, and help people to answer questions like this: Is it right for a Government, white or black, to practise crude racial discrimination? Is it right for part of the world to be complacent about its own prosperity while other parts of the world have hunger and starvation? Is it right to try to solve a grievance by violence? Is it right to pollute the atmosphere? Again and again the answer is bound up with some belief which Christians hold about God, about Man or about the world.

How does the Church bear this witness? In part, but only in part, by the Church's leaders saying things. In part, and a very large part, by Christians who live in difficult situations doing the right thing. Then there is need to create opinion through Christians together showing that something is utterly contrary to the Christian way of life. But all the time it is supremely important for the Church not to be a set of people with negative things to say, don't do this or don't do that, but a set of people who point to Jesus Christ himself. Show us Jesus, that is Man's greatest need. Show us Jesus, and he will be the inspiration, the challenge and the goal. Show us God himself in his greatness and goodness, for there alone is the true perspective for Man's life.

Part Two: Learning to Live

The Bible as a Means of Grace

THE ARCHBISHOP OF YORK

The Bible is a dated book; or more accurately, a little library of dated books. How could it be otherwise? The most recent of the books was written nearly 1900 years ago; the most ancient, many centuries earlier than that. It tells, in picture language, of the beginning of things, of primitive times and ancient love stories, of battles long ago. It is a strange mixture of poetry and prose, of parables and letters, of prophecy and history.

How, then, can it be included in a series of things designated as 'Means of Grace', a phrase which I take it is meant to indicate ways by which God comes through to men in power and love? The Eucharist? Yes. Prayer? Yes. But the Bible?

The fact is that it has proved just that – a means of grace – to men and women of all kinds down the long centuries, and still is just that to millions today. This in spite of modern man having 'come of age', as the saying goes; in spite of his being a highly sophisticated, scientifically orientated creature, so very different in many ways from those who wrote the Bible and from those for whom it was originally intended.

What is the explanation of this undoubted fact? It lies, I think, partly in this – that the Bible is very largely a book of biography; it consists of life stories of men and women looked at as individuals and as members of communities. It is true that we humans change from century to century in many respects; for example, men who lived before the discovery of the wheel were very different from those, like ourselves, who live in the space age. Yet, beneath these surface differences lie certain characteristics which do not change from millennium to millennium: our need for love, for forgiveness, for happy community relations, for light on the basic problems of human existence and on life after death, and so on.

Another reason why this ancient book, dated as it undoubtedly is, seems to transcend the centuries and becomes a means of grace to modern man is this: it talks about God. Indeed this is the main burden of its message. From one point of view, it is the story of Man's search for God – and there *are* parts of that search-story which, in the full light of the Christian revelation, do not prove very edifying or enlightening. But, from a much more important angle, the Bible can be viewed as the age-long story of God's search for Man – 'Adam, where art thou?' *Here* lies the permanent value of the Bible, for Christians believe that God is still on the search for Man, and that his great heart of love is not satisfied till Man comes to himself and comes to his Father, and so finds rest in God.

That much must be said by way of introduction. The Bible is a book which speaks to men of different ages and backgrounds. Perhaps we should more accurately say that the Bible is a book through which, as through no other book, the Spirit of the living God speaks to men, under the widely varying conditions in which they find themselves. Coleridge used to say that it has a way of 'finding' the devout reader of its pages. That's not a bad way of putting it.

So, in the next four talks, we shall take different instances of how God does this; we shall look at different circumstances in which Man finds himself and in which the Bible has a relevant word to speak. If we illustrate what we have to say pretty frequently from human experience, that will not be surprising, for the simple reason we have already noted that the Bible is full of biographical material. We shall soon see how the Bible speaks to us in times of crisis, when we are in need of guidance.

In Times of Crisis

There have been some, in days gone by, who have looked on the Bible rather as a book of charms, from which guidance can be extracted, by a kind of lucky dip system, in times of crisis, emergency, or uncertainty. They open the Bible at random and hope that, by a sort of supernatural good luck, their eye will light on a passage which will give them the direction they need. Maybe God is good enough to overlook the immaturity of his servants and sometimes to answer their hopes in this way. For myself, I put little trust in it.

But how often we do need guidance. Has the Bible anything to say about how to get it? Yes, I think so. Let's look at two people who have something to say on the matter.

The first was a king who lived in the Near East in the eighth century before Christ. His nation was a small one; his temporal power was not very great. Power rested in the hands of the great nations which lay to the North and East of his land of Israel, nations like Assyria. It was from Assyria that he received one day a letter couched in terms that would make any king tremble for the safety of his people and his throne. It was a mocking letter: 'Don't start bragging about the power of your God to deliver you from my hand! Look at the other nations which I have subdued. What has happened to them? Of what avail were their prayers to their gods? You had better learn your lesson and submit, before I crush you.'

It was a terrible ultimatum. Great issues were at stake.

How the king, Hezekiah, needed the guidance of God!

This is what he did. He took the letter from the hand of the messengers who had brought it. He read it. He went up to the temple of the Lord and spread it out before the Lord, and poured his heart out in prayer. The details of how God answered that prayer through the prophet Isaiah need not concern us now. But the action of Hezekiah certainly has got a lesson if we are trying to see how God gives guidance on important occasions.

It would have been possible for him to rush into battle in a fury at the cheek of the King of Assyria. It would have been possible for him to submit, or to flee from his post of responsibility. He did none of these things. Quietly he laid the matter before God – and waited. He did not wait in vain. No rush, no panic, but *prayer*. That is how the guidance came.

The second person who learnt the way of divine guidance was Jesus Christ himself. There are indications in the Gospels that, before he made great decisions, he would withdraw from the bustle of the town and from the pressure of the crowds, and wait on God in the quiet of the country. He did this, for example, before he chose his twelve closest followers, the apostles. So much hung on this decision. He would not rush into it. He must seek the mind of his Father unhurriedly. He must ask him for his guidance in the intimacy of dialogue, in prayer. These men were to be the leaders of his mission in the months and years ahead. 'Father, show me your mind'.

As we read between the lines of the Gospels, we see a kind of rhythm in the life of Jesus. Nature has its rhythms, the rhythms of the seasons and the tides; the rhythms of sleeping and waking; the rhythms of withdrawal and activity. So it seems to have been in the life of Jesus, planned with a kind of magisterial serenity: activity preceded by prayer; preaching, healing and teaching following quiet communion with his Father.

It was in this way, I believe, that Jesus may well have come to rely less and less on sudden revelations of guidance from God in times of emergency. By constantly repeated acts of communion with God, he learnt the principles on which God runs his world and seeks to guide his children. When the crisis came, he knew which way to go.

In Times of Celebration

There's a strange idea about that the Bible is a sombre book. In the old days it used to be bound in black, and printed in small type; and that helped to convey this impression of gloom. Of course, it does deal with the serious side of human experience. It deals with sin and disease and death; with temptation and doubt and darkness. It wouldn't be a very realistic book if it hadn't got a lot to say on these things. But, has it got anything to say to those for whom life is *good?* Can it be a 'means of grace' at a time of joy and celebrations? The answer most certainly is 'Yes, it can'.

The central rite of Christian worship is the Eucharist. The word simply means 'Thanksgiving'. When the Church 'does this in remembrance' of its crucified and risen Lord, it engages in a 'celebration', a joyful feast. It uses wine, the symbol of gladness and warmth and cheer. Though that wine speaks of the blood of Christ outpoured in sacrificial giving, it also speaks of exuberant joy.

The story of the turning of the water into wine at the wedding feast in Cana of Galilee was the writer's way of saying that, when Jesus is present and his will is obeyed, there is festival, there is fun, there is something to sing about, something to celebrate.

There is evidence in the Gospels which leads us to think

that Jesus had pondered a great deal on the book of Deuteronomy. Now that isn't the first book which you would turn up if you wanted to understand the Bible and you went to it as a comparative beginner. By no means! But it has some very interesting things to say. For instance, if you were to open it at the fourteenth chapter, you would find a passage which might not interest you particularly, all about animals and birds that you may or may not eat; a sort of primitive list of health-food laws. But that passage is followed by one which might be headed: 'How to enjoy a celebration, a jollification'. It's a description of a kind of super harvest festival, a grand feast or, if that were to prove impossible, a grand spending spree. No suggestion here that the people of God are spoil-sports, or dismal folk ruled by negatives, 'thou shalt not, thou shalt not, thou shalt not'. No, there seems to be a foretaste of what a New Testament writer was later to lay down as a kind of manifesto for positive Christian living: 'God has given us richly all things to enjoy'. Here is a life-affirming principle which has not always been followed by the disciples of the One who sometimes seemed more at home, more comfortable, with the worldly types of his day than he did with religious, sour-faced rigorists.

If you look a bit more closely at that passage in Deuteronomy on how to enjoy a celebration, you will find two very interesting things about it. The first is that it is all done 'before the Lord'. That does not mean that God looks down with a disapproving eye when life is going well with us and we want to celebrate. Not at all. It simply means that we conduct our jollifications, as we seek to conduct all aspects of life (business, leisure, love, the lot), in the way that he approves, or, to use the accepted religious phrase, 'to his glory'.

The other thing of interest about this passage is that strict instructions are given not to forget the under-privileged, the people less fortunate, the socially deprived. The equivalent today would be those who have slipped through the provisions made by the Welfare Services – and we always have such among us – and, looking further afield, the millions in the Third World. While they are around, extravagance is obscene.

The Lord who entered into the joys of the wedding feast and made them infinitely greater by his presence and his action, loves to enter into our celebrations, to share with us when life is good and skies are blue. At the same time, he reminds us of those for whom there is little joy in life, little to celebrate. And he once told a story which illustrated the fact that a man *can* get so obsessed with celebrations, with wealth and all that goes with it, that the seed of eternal life gets choked. And that is disaster beyond all telling.

In Times of Sickness

It's a pretty safe bet that, among those listening to Thought for the Day on any morning, there are a good many thousands of people who are ill, or who have in the past experienced illness of mind or body. Very few of us get through life without some experience of sickness of some sort. The body – and even more the mind – is a wonderful and complicated machine. The surprise is that it doesn't get out of order more often than it does.

The Bible is a very down-to-earth book, and it has a lot to say about the body. The writers refuse to think of Man as 'a soul' (important) encased in 'a body' (unimportant). They will not divide us up like that. They think of us as persons, our bodies being very much part of our 'personalities'. The body is a God-given part of us, not to be pampered, but to be treated with reverence as a temple of the Holy Spirit. That is why self-indulgence of any kind is blasphemous.

Speaking broadly, one can say that the God of the Bible is a God who is on the side of health, of wholeness. Quite a large part of the opening books of the Old Testament is given over to laws, including food-laws, which have to do with health, sanitation, sex-relationships, and so on. The body, and the happy relationship of mind and body, and the interrelationships of people within the body corporate, *matter* to the God of the Bible.

But it is when we come to the Gospels that we see things most clearly, and so the Bible becomes a means of grace to all of us who suffer. Not that a reading of the Gospels clears up all the problems about suffering. Let me be frank and say quite openly that it hasn't done that for me. But it has shed some rays of clear and penetrating light on the problem, and given me enough to go on with.

The Gospels show me our Lord as a fighter on behalf of health. How he wrestled with disease, curing the woman with the crooked back ('whom Satan has bound these 18 years'); the paralytic on his stretcher-bed (whose paralysis seemed closely linked with his sinfulness); the mentally tortured man (whose nickname Legion spoke only too eloquently of his tormented disintegration). Jesus lined himself up with all those who are fighting for health; but he refused to deal only with the outward symptoms. He insisted on getting at the cause. He refused to say that suffering was always the direct result of the sufferer's sin; that would have been far too much of an over-simplification. But he recognised the interaction of evil and bodily and mental sickness, and allowed full scope for that in his healing work.

We never read that Jesus was ill. We read that he was tired, that strength went out of him in the course of his work, and so on; but not that he was ill during the course of his ministry. Perhaps it was that he was in such close touch with the God of peace and health that God's wholeness became the wholeness of his Son. What we *do* read, however, is this: on the Cross there came to him such an experience of agony – physical, mental, spiritual agony – as has been the lot of no other. Here was a young man, at the height of his powers, nailed through feet and hands to a beam of wood, his dreams shattered round him, forsaken, so it seemed, by his God and by his friends. It was a bloody agony; all the misdeeds of the world seemed centred, that awful day, in that torn body. 'My God, my God, *why* . . .?'

He did not escape from suffering, nor do we. But he took it and made something wonderful of it. He transformed it; and through his wounds mankind is healed. His love in the midst of his suffering changed the meaning of events, made the ugly things beautiful and the hard things acceptable. Two pieces of wood became the symbol of salvation; a crown of thorns his halo; Golgotha his throne of glory.

Let me put it this way. When suffering hits us, it is natural enough to ask the question 'Why?' Jesus did. But it is more important to ask the question 'How? How will God make this thing, which to me is so negative, into a plus in his hands? Is it possible that I am on my back so that I may learn to look up?' That might be the most wonderful thing I could do.

An unknown soldier in the American Civil War wrote these words:

> I asked God for strength, that I might achieve;
> I was made weak, that I might learn humbly to obey.
> I asked for health, that I might do greater things;
> I was given infirmity, that I might do better things.
> I asked for power, that I might have the praise of
>   men;

I was given weakness, that I might face the need
of God.

In Times when The World seems to have Gone Mad

Some centuries before Christ was born, a man looked out over his world. He had, of course, no radio or television as we have, no newspapers even, to bring that world into his living-room and keep him informed from hour to hour of its goings-on. But such news as he got – through passing camel cavalcades and couriers and swiftly spreading rumours – convinced him that it was a mad, mad world. The very mountains seemed to shake and, as he put it, the waters seemed to rage and swell. It was like a volcanic eruption. The little land he lived in had proved all too often in past history to be the place over which the great powers fought; his people were a kind of pawn in the unscrupulous hands of competing nations round about. What could a man say, what could he do, where could he find confidence in a world like *that?*

We don't know the name of the man we've been talking about, but from the poem he wrote we can deduce a good deal about him. He was very much a man of the world; he kept his eyes open and, as we say, 'he knew a thing or two'. But his vision was not confined to what his physical eyes saw about him. He was a man of faith. He had an answer to the question as to where his confidence could be found in a world gone mad. '*God* is our hope and strength,' he said; 'a very present help in time of trouble. Therefore we will not fear, though the earth be moved . . .' So he kept quiet, and listened; and as he listened, strength began to take the place of fear. He heard God speaking: 'Be still,' he said, 'and know that I am God.'

The writings of those unknown men who wrote the

psalms breathe a superb confidence. 'God reigns,' they say again and again. God has not abdicated, even though men seem to have gone mad. God reigns. God loves. God cares.

Men like these, with their strong note of confidence, can become a 'means of grace' to us who live in even more troubled days than were theirs. Our days hold within them possibilities of disaster (nuclear and the like) which they never dreamed of, and instances of human folly which never occurred to them.

There are many today who are appalled by human insanity and by Man's inhumanity to Man, and all the more appalled because they feel that they can do so little about it. They do not occupy the seats of power; their word avails little; they seem to be very small cogs in a vast impersonal machine. Perhaps this is especially true of the shut-ins, whose main life-work is behind them. They read the papers and find their stories depressing; they listen in and find the news to be little more than a series of disasters. To such people I want to say two things:

First, remember where the Psalmists put their trust. Remember that a greater than the Psalmist, Jesus Christ himself, dared, in the face of all the terrors of his day, to call God Father and King. A Father who seeks the love of His children; a King who seeks their loyalty and obedience. Jesus dared to hold, in life and in death, that God reigns; that he loves; that he cares.

Secondly, remember that God is not dependent on the big battalions to do his work. He has a way of working through minority groups, or even through individuals, undistinguished people, even through men and women who are unconscious of being agents of his power. This means that *you*, far though you are from what most people conceive of as the corridors of power, can be a centre of serenity in a world that seems to have gone mad. If the room where you live becomes a place of prayer, it may be more potent for good than the council-chambers of the nations' potentates.

BISHOP B. C. BUTLER

Prayer: to Whom?

Do you ever want to 'get away from it all'? That is a phrase that we sometimes hear on the lips of others, even if not within our own heart. What is the 'it' from which people wish to get away? It is the almost unbearable tangle of work and pleasure – so-called – and personal relations and obligations and duties of various kinds, yes, and pains and sorrows, that bear in on us with their tangible presence and clamour and give us a sense of being caught in a spider's web that is strangling the life within us. We suffer from a kind of claustrophobia. We want to escape.

But where are we to escape to? Wherever we go, we find that the spider's web, some other sector of it which we perhaps had not suspected to exist before, is there before us. And wherever we go, we carry with us the tangle that is our own selves. Like the things and persons that surround us, our own self has little areas which, taken separately, seem to make sense. But the whole of it adds up to – what? We are tempted to say: to one total absurdity.

Of course, life and reality would be totally absurd were it not for God. Or rather, there could not be any life, any reality, unless God were sustaining us and our world from moment to moment in the embrace of his wisdom, his power, his love. If the force of gravity were suddenly to cease, our physical universe would fall apart. Without God, our whole universe could not survive for a moment. All beauty, all goodness, all brilliance of invention and integrity of thought, have their source in him; all value, and all being.

Perhaps our dissatisfaction with our life and world, our desire to get away from it all, when it is not just a passing mood, is due to the fact that we leave God out of our concern. You don't have to pay much serious attention to the scientific truth of gravity; you have only to behave as if gravity were a fact – without thinking about it – and then your walking and climbing and jumping and diving can go on as usual. But God is not a scientific law. He is a personal – or rather a more than personal – reality of infinite richness and inexhaustible mystery of delight. If you utterly fail to try to relate to a person, that person becomes less and less important, less and less helpful, in your life.

Prayer, which is my subject in these talks, is much more than just asking God for favours – like the schoolboy cricketer who prayed to God for rain to assist his bowling, and was greeted by a cloud-burst. To ask God for what we want is a perfectly sensible kind of behaviour; after all, we are taught to regard him as our heavenly Father, and children are frank with their parents about what they want. But a child who never opened his mouth except to ask for things would be rather a bore.

Some people think that prayer is just a childish way of comforting oneself, a phoney bit of auto-suggestion. That is what it would be if we believed that there is no God. But if God is real (and he is real) then by prayer we get into personal relations with him. When in prayer we ask for blessings, of course he already knows our needs. To pray to him is to make that knowledge something held in common between him and us.

Prayer, as I use the word, stands for all our developing personal relations with God. As it is with those we love on earth, so too with God: by developing relations, exploring methods of communication with him, we grow to love him more, and he comes to mean more to us. And as he comes to mean more to us, so too do our world and our life, even our very selves, come to mean more to us. They reveal more of their unplumbed depths of richness and beauty and goodness. They fall into place, as physical objects are ranged in their places by gravity. And we no longer want to get away from it all, because in, and through, and so beyond, it all we are growing into union with him who is our lodestar, the magnetic north which draws us always towards himself, but will not effectively draw us unless we consent, by prayer, to be drawn.

Father of the Family

A little girl, so the story goes, was absorbed with paper and crayon, drawing something. 'What are you drawing today?' her mother asked her. 'God,' was the short reply. Slightly shocked, her mother said: 'But you can't *draw* God, darling; no one knows what God looks like.' 'They will soon,' said the little girl, and went on with her drawing.

God is the ultimate mystery, the unbounded deep of which the poet speaks, from which all things come and whither all things, and we among them, tend.

What is he like? Like the little girl of the story, mankind has for ever been trying to picture God. The results have sometimes been strange. There have been caricatures of God. He has been thought of as an arbitrary tyrant, inventing senseless rules for his creatures beyond their power to obey. God, or 'the gods' have been represented in animal shapes and worshipped with cruel sacrifices. Often one can say to a man: tell me what 'your' God is like, and I shall know what you are like yourself. The Jewish religion had good reason for forbidding any pictorial representation of God at all.

Yet there is something in Man's make-up which cannot

rest content with treating the notion of God as an empty term with no meaning that we can assign to it at all.

Christians turn to Jesus Christ for help in this need. Jesus has his own 'picture' of God. God is his 'heavenly Father', and Jesus teaches his followers to pray to God as *their* Father: 'Our Father who art in heaven.' It is picture language, of course. 'Heaven' originally meant what we call the sky, and God does not dwell in the sky in any sense in which he does not also dwell in the ocean, in the atoms, in and beyond and in another dimension from the vast expanses of time and space opened up for us by modern science. When we address God as our father *in heaven*, we mean that he is our father in an absolute sense; not limited like any earthly father. And of course this means that the word 'father' itself, when we use it of God, is picture language. God is far more than anything that we can conceive by the word father. He is more wise, more powerful, more loving, than the earthly father of any child. And so, as the child responds to his earthly father with complete admiration, trust and love, so – but more so – we respond to God in admiration – adoration – trust and love.

An earthly family is a community of love. We don't only show our love for our parents by direct relations with them. We show our love for them in our love and helpfulness towards our brothers and sisters, whom we know to be as dear to our parents as we ourselves are.

So we love God by loving our fellow human beings, knowing that he is their father as much as he is ours. No one who loves his heavenly father can be content till, with the help of his own efforts where they can be of use, his fellow-men's needs are met. It is one of the great Christian truths that you cannot love God whom you have not seen unless you love your human brother whom you have seen. We could call our service of God in the service of our fellow-men a form of indirect prayer.

But a child who only played with his brothers and sisters and never had a word for his parents would be failing in love for his father and mother. So besides indirect prayer there is direct prayer. Jesus didn't only teach his disciples. He prayed to his heavenly father directly, and in prayer, even in his agony, he expressed his complete trust in him. 'Let this cup of suffering pass from me; nevertheless, not my will be done but yours.'

Prayer then, direct and indirect, is the loving practice of a direct relationship with God who loves us and who will find his own way, mysteriously, of speaking to us as we try to develop our loving prayer, our side of the personal relationship that links us with him.

The Adventure of Prayer

Man is born to live in society and to share with others not only in the material things of life but in art and music and poetry and the things of the spirit. So prayer is not only something that we each do separately apart from everyone else. A philosopher once said that religion is 'what a man does with his solitude', but this is not completely true. As we share together in sport and culture, so we come together to share in prayer and worship. A Christian is a member of a great family or communion of other Christians. We share common concerns and we express the heart of our faith in common worship.

Many experiments are being made today in the matter of common worship – too many for the comfort of some Christians, who are homesick for the old familiar ways. The great Churches of the Western world, whether Catholic or Anglican or Protestant, are the fields for such experimenting. But much of it goes on outside the limits of what you could call the official worship of these churches. There are prayer groups springing up, particularly among the young. There is what is now called charismatic renewal – I apologise for the term – or what is known as a new kind of Pentecostalism. These modern movements, in my opinion, are neither to be simply condemned nor welcomed without any criticism or reservation. At least we can rejoice that so many people are beginning to realise afresh that Christianity without prayer is a body without a soul.

In these talks I am concentrating on personal rather than corporate prayer and worship. After all, corporate worship itself, unless it is inspired by the personal self-committal and engagement of those who take part in it, is just an empty formalism or an arid task to be fulfilled out of obedience to Church law. Only personal engagement can breathe the spirit of life into it.

Personal prayer is most itself when it is most spontaneous. We can be moved to such prayer by all sorts of things and situations: a beautiful scene that calls forth our praise of the God of nature; human disaster or distress, which arouses our compassion and makes us turn to the heavenly Father who is the source of all help and comfort; or again, the need to make some important decision which leads us to ask the help of the Holy Spirit of God; or a sudden realisation of our own moral or religious failures which leads us to turn to him for forgiveness and grace. I suppose that it is typical of the saints that, when the pressure of passing preoccupations is relieved for a moment, their hearts turn, like a compass needle, towards God who is our ultimate point of reference.

But we are not all saints, though we are called to be saints. Nearly all of us need to have a simple rule of prayer. If we don't deliberately arrange for intervals of prayer in our life, the impulse to spontaneous prayer will probably fade and decay.

A 'rule of prayer'. This may sound formidable, but I don't mean it to be such. We can easily make up our minds that every morning, before we go down to breakfast and begin to get involved in the life of the world, we will spend a minute or two in prayer. We can use this very brief time to thank God for looking after us, to ask for his help in the coming day, and to offer ourselves to him to be used by him as he sees fit in the hours that lie ahead of us.

In the same way, we can arrange that at night, before we get into bed, we will similarly give a minute or two to God; during which we can thank him for keeping us safe during the day, for all the blessings and joys of the day, and just for being our heavenly Father. We can ask him to forgive our failures during the day. And we can ask him to bless and keep in his care those who are dear to us and to help all those in need and distress.

Two Masters?

Laurence van der Post, in his book about the Bushman of South Africa, tells how he came to make the journey of exploration on which this book is based. He had had the idea of such a journey when he was a boy. But it was many years later that it began to revive in him again. He tried to persuade other people to undertake the exploration, but gradually he began to feel, against his conscious will, that perhaps he should do it himself. 'Then one morning,' he says, 'I awoke to find that, in sleep, my mind had been decided for me. "I will go and find the Bushman," I told myself, suddenly amazed that so simple a statement had never presented itself to me before.'

Prayer can be viewed as a journey to discover God. We all know that the journey is possible. We know, vaguely perhaps, that without God nothing else is worth while. Perhaps when we were young we decided that when we were grown up we would undertake the journey. Then of course other things came to preoccupy us: 'Worldly cares and the glamour of wealth' choked the word of God. Well, not perhaps the glamour of wealth but the hard business of life and the fascination of our surroundings.

But anyone who tries to pray, however half-heartedly, is leaving a chink in his armour through which the arrow of God's grace may find its way. Gradually, we may find ourselves saying once more to ourselves: Really, there is nothing which could compare with the real adventure, the real challenge, of seriously seeking to grow closer to God. That is what the saints through the ages have done; and someone once said: The only sad thing is, not to be a saint. Well, we should perhaps laugh at the idea that we are really ourselves called to be saints. Still, God is real enough; and our half-hearted prayers have half-heartedly acknowledged the fact. And if God is real, he is supremely worth while. And we have an absolute guarantee that, if we will seek him, we shall find him. We find ourselves being driven spiritually into a corner, from which there is no way out except by deciding, like van der Post: 'I will go and find God'.

Such a simple decision. As easy as opening an unlocked door in front of us. But it's a revolutionary decision. It means that we shall be arranging our life henceforward so that God is not just fitted into the bits of time that we cannot usefully employ on other matters. Prayer will become the central concern, around which everything else will have to take its place. Instead of making room in our life for prayer, we shall be seeing things the other way round: How can I organise my days so that the claims of this world, lawful as they are, will become secondary to my love-affair with God?

Because that's what prayer is, when it really takes the

central place. A love-affair with God, infinitely exciting, growing and deepening as the weeks and months pass by, like a human love-affair which may become less frantic as the years go on, but which grows ever deeper until I can say: My true love has my heart and I have his. To be really in love with God is not necessarily a very emotional affair, but it can become very engrossing. It's a bit like music. Most of us have some interest in music. Some people have this interest to such an extent that music becomes their life. When prayer becomes one's life, one is at least on the road that the greatest followers of Christ have followed. We may wonder how far we shall get on that road; but the important thing is to be going along it. It is the road he himself took; and his call to those who listen to him is: Follow me.

Good Friday and Easter

The Christian does not only learn from the teaching of Jesus Christ. It is true that from that teaching he learns the supremely important truth that God is 'our heavenly Father', that in fact God is pure love, and that all that happens to us, however hard to interpret, is in fact the touch of his loving hand upon us.

But the New Testament does not only present Jesus Christ to us as a true teacher. It tells us that Jesus is himself the revelation, the self-disclosure, the self-giving, of God: 'He that has seen me has seen the Father;' or again, 'Blessed are the eyes that see what you see, for many prophets and wise men have desired to see what you see and have not seen it.' So for Christians the life of Jesus Christ, and its triumph in his resurrection on the first Easter day, is an entry into the very heart of the mystery of God. It is also, since he was God disclosed in human terms, the very model of the life in which prayer and living are one.

At first sight the life of Jesus seems to have been one of almost ceaseless activity and involvement in the world about him. A life of talking and teaching and religious controversy. But all this was undergirded by his prayer. We can take one episode as typical. St Mark's Gospel, perhaps putting into a single day the contents of several occasions, tells us how Jesus, one Sabbath, taught in the synagogue and there worked a miracle which left his audience dumbfounded. He then went to the house of St Peter, where he cured Peter's mother-in-law. The same day after sunset 'the whole town was there, gathered at the door' of Peter's house, and he healed the sick people whom they had brought to him (it must have been a very busy day indeed). Yet 'very early next morning' he got up and went out to a lonely spot 'and remained there in prayer'. Prayer, I think, was the undercurrent of his life; and it was prayer that impelled him to his ceaseless activity.

Christians like other people look for success. We want to see our efforts for the conversion and improvement of the world bearing visible fruit. We want our prayer-life, by which all our other efforts are inspired, to develop and to bring us consciously closer to God; we want to 'experience God'.

Yet the point about the life of Jesus as the New Testament puts it before us is that his life was a failure. He had received from his heavenly Father a mission to raise God's own people, the Jewish people, to a new height of religion and of faith. He did have some small success and gathered a group of disciples around him. But on the wider stage of history he failed and was disowned by the official representatives of his own people. When the final crisis came he was betrayed by one of his closest disciples; the others forsook him and fled. As for his prayer life: well, on the night in which he was betrayed and arrested we see him in agony, begging his heavenly

Father to be spared what he saw before him; but the prayer was not answered in the way he had asked it: he had to go through with the treachery and the mockery and the awful physical and mental pain 'even to the death on the cross'. And on the cross itself, he is depicted as crying out to his heavenly Father: 'My God, my God, why have you left me in the lurch?'

Christian life and prayer are not promised success as the world reckons success. Success came to Jesus, of course, but it was the success 'beyond this world' of a resurrection of which we know by faith. So my last remark about prayer is: don't be surprised if things are not as easy as you would like. Don't give up even when the whole enterprise seems to be a failure. The resurrection of Christ is the anchor of our faith and the source of our hope. Apparent failure is more than worth while, for it leads on to a triumph beyond our understanding. 'Fear not,' says Jesus to each one of us, 'for I have overcome the world.' And St John says that the Christian victory is 'our faith'.

MICHAEL MARSHALL

The Bread of Revolution

Jesus took the bread, gave thanks for it, broke it and gave it and said: 'This is me. This is my life and this is your life and this is what life is all about'.

That revolution we have tamed, reduced and sadly impoverished, turning a manifesto for life into a pious observance. 'What time is the early service? Oh, eight o'clock.' But that 'early service' – that Holy Communion – is the Eucharist, the 'thanksgiving', and it is intended to open up a whole new way of life for man. It was intended to change the living death of our materialistic, grabbing world into a new and living world, which really could become God's world in time and for eternity.

For, you see, this day belongs to God. Life itself belongs to God, and that means that it is not your property and it is not mine. It's only when we begin to see life as it is – a gift, unearned, unmanufactured – that we can really begin to enjoy and to be free from it, free really to begin at all.

But we get hold of the wrong end of the stick. In fact, we get hold of life in the wrong way altogether. We get it the wrong way round. There's nothing worse than someone who patronises his parents, and so there's nothing worse than when a creature plays at being the creator. He ravages the world and begins to treat it as though it belonged to him, as though life owed him something, as though it were his life and he was going to live it. 'This is my life and I'm going to do what I want with it. This is my body and I'm going to do as I want with it.' It's a kind of theft and robbery, and it's not long before it's robbery with violence.

The manifesto of Christ's revolution was intended to turn that sort of attitude right round, to turn us inside out and to turn the world upside down. For the truth is the very opposite. Life is a gift. Everything and everyone is a gift. Life owes me nothing: it is a free gift, unearned, unmerited. 'Everything comes from you, O God, and of your own do we give you.'

And until we get things the right way round, the world itself will never go round. That is the only revolution which will end all other revolutions, but such a revolution requires that we break with a whole outlook on life, a whole attitude to the world around us. It involves a change of attitude to our environment, to the raw materials of the earth. We have got to begin to take life – everything in life – as Jesus took that piece of bread, and discover how it can be turned from the sort of possession which possesses us into the kind of gift which refreshes and liberates us. We were intended by God to be masters of his world but instead we have ended up becoming slaves of what we like to call our world, possessed by possessions, longing to belong, but in fact alienated and belonging only to our belongings.

'Thank you' – just that one word – makes the world of difference: oh, not just in grace muttered before meals (though that's a start even over a quick morning cup of tea, or the morning's breakfast) but with everything. Yes, I mean everything. This day belongs to God: 'This is the day that the Lord has made, I will rejoice and be glad in it'.

Jesus started a revolution with a piece of bread, but like all revolutions it cannot stop there. His intention is to take your life and mine, and transform it, consecrate it, radically change it. But it all starts with a new outlook, getting things the right way round. Life is a gift, not a reward or what I deserve. It is a privilege, not a right. And there's only one response to that way of seeing things. Thank you. Thank you again and again.

The Bread of Life

The revolution which we like to call the communion service is a whole way of life. It becomes debased into a superstition if we reduce it to a discussion simply about what happens to that piece of bread. But if on the other hand we take seriously what Jesus did with that piece of bread, then the communion service becomes uncomfortably relevant, and the key to what life is all about. What happens to that piece of bread was also the story of his own life and it becomes the story of your life and mine. There are only three miracles which really matter in the world, and they are all to do with the Body of Christ. The first is how on earth God could possibly take a human body at all, bless it, be broken in it and give himself through it for the life of the world? That is the life of Jesus, the Body of Christ in Palestine, two thousand years ago.

But that's only the beginning. There's a second miracle. How on earth can ordinary men and women be taken by God, blessed, broken and given, and become vehicles of eternal charity? For that's what your life and mine are all about, the Body of Christ in Piccadilly Circus.

And there's that third miracle. How on earth can a piece of bread be taken, blessed, broken and given and become the life of Jesus, the Body of Christ? But that's what the world is all about: the Body of Christ in every atom, every grain of sand and in all matter.

But the first question is the same with all three of those miracles. Could he take it? Can we take it? He took it all right, uncompromising, no holds barred. God became man and took our flesh, our lives; he took what was there, a body, a piece of bread and there were no 'ifs' and 'buts'. Always he took life as it came and that is the first step in growing up at all. So many of us spend our days looking the gift horse of life in the mouth. 'If only I had a different job; if only I lived somewhere else; if only I had better looks; better parents . . .' Yes, we commit spiritual suicide every day of our lives.

Can you take it? Because until you can take it as a raw material gift, you will never change it. Just take your hand and look at it. There's not another exactly like that in the whole world; a unique combination of strength and weakness, brilliance and stupidity. That's your fingerprint, that is your life. Take hold of it and thank God for it – all of it I mean, the good and the bad. 'Blessed are you Lord God of all creation. Through your goodness we have this bread to offer. Bread which earth has given and human hands have made. It will become the Bread of Life.' That is what is said as the bread is placed on the altar at communion. And that is the first step towards consecration and transformation. For if we are to grow up at all and break through the living death of life, we must learn to take our lives as he took his body and he took the bread: 'for better, for worse, for richer, for poorer, in sickness and in health'. Then at least one miracle has begun today. That unqualified acceptance of life is the beginning of the miracle of growth and transformation. Like 'Beauty and the Beast', the Beast must be embraced if it is ever to become the Prince Charming.

For that is how Jesus embraced the human race. That's how he took hold of the bread, and, strengthened with that same Bread of Life, that is how we must take hold of our lives, others' lives and today. One of the great Christian Fathers says, 'What he did not take, he did not redeem'. What we cannot take cannot be redeemed.

'Take my life and let it be consecrated, Lord, to thee.' A communion service? Yes, but much more than that. A whole way of life. This is *your* life. Can you take it?

The Bread of Thanksgiving

At the Supper, Jesus took bread for blessing: we so often take it for granted. How often a marriage begins to go wrong when one of the partners starts to take the other for granted. Such an attitude to another person is destructive of true relationships. No matter how well you know someone, you can never afford to take them for granted.

So Jesus took the bread – as he did everything else in life – and gave thanks for it; he blessed it. He did not take it for granted, he took it and gave thanks for it. He did this because he saw that not only the bread but the whole of life is an unearned gift. So whatever flaws, failings and imperfections he saw, the basic attitude of Jesus in life was an attitude of thankfulness. In fact it's fair to say that his habit of taking bread and giving thanks for it was a typical characteristic which was recognisable and distinctive. It gave the show away when the risen Jesus walked with his disciples to Emmaus, and at first they did not recognise him. But once they sat down at supper and he took hold of that bread, raised his eyes to heaven and gave thanks, they knew all right who it was. But the attitude which underlies that action turns the whole of life inside out. With that attitude, I cease to talk about my rights: I have none. In fact, I can literally thank God that man does not get what he deserves. God's gifts, like the rain and the sunshine, are scattered carelessly everywhere, free for all. But if I am to receive those gifts, and if they are to flourish in my life, then I must change my attitude to life. I must learn to say thank you.

The holy communion service is sometimes called the Eucharist which just means 'thanksgiving'. It is not just a church service, but an attitude to the whole of life, an attitude which cuts right across our materialistic world. Furthermore, that attitude is the second step in the right direction: take it and give thanks for it. Do not take it and take it for granted. Give thanks for it 'at all times and in all places'. For there is no time and no place outside God's providence; there is no situation on earth where it is not possible to do God's will. The Christian attitude is not to go looking for goldmines, but to take the mud and turn it to gold.

Because in the end there are only two attitudes to life: thanking which is blessing, or taking life for granted which ends up cursing. It's no use just going to Holy Communion resentful of others, resentful of life, of old age, of retirement, of being passed over for promotion, or it will be a lie and no true Eucharist. Jesus tells us, in those situations, 'Go and first be reconciled'. Change your attitude. Of course I can think of some terrible situations where it is very difficult indeed to be thankful. But you know that is the only attitude which will actually change the situation, and change the world. Imagine what it can feel like when Christians exchange what they call 'the kiss of peace'. You happen to be sitting next to someone you can't stand, a Samaritan; you'd rather be dead than be seen with *him*. Now turn to him in the Communion for the 'kiss of peace'. Embrace him, greet him, shake him by the hand. Yes, that kind of religion can be very uncomfortable. It makes a difference.

'Heaven and earth are full of your glory', but my goodness it needs unlocking and the key is a word: thank you. Finally, a prayer of George Herbert: 'Thou hast given so much to us, give one thing more, a grateful heart; for Christ's sake. Amen.'

The Bread of Sacrifice

The bread of the Eucharist is what life is all about. I can't explain why a good God allows suffering in the world. What I can tell you is that I shall never really grow up until I've been *through* it, been broken and suffered: until I have had my heart broken, just like that piece of bread. Broken in two, just like the heart of Jesus.

True life is true loving. But true loving is unconditional acceptance and thankfulness. Start to love like that and you're bound to be broken before long. The cosmic process of consecration involves your life and mine, just as much as that piece of bread in the Holy Communion; and both alike are part of that same process in which Jesus himself is broken. That is true communion. And I don't know any other way of growing up, which is why at every communion service we are invited to lift up our hearts. We offer back to God, literally, 'what makes us tick', the things we love most, the people we love most. For these are the very things we need freeing from, our children, our jobs and ambitions, our possessions and the things we've lost our hearts to. These are the wonderful gifts of God, but unless we can let go of them – break with them – they will break us and we shall break them. If we do not lift up our hearts, we shall lose our hearts.

And the pattern is always the same. It's the oldest story in the world. Abraham and his wife wanted a son but she was past it. But then their prayer was answered and an angel came to tell Abraham that Sarah would bear a son. She just got a fit of the giggles when she heard this news, but sure enough they had a son all right – an only son, an only child, their heart's desire, born of old parents. They called him Isaac. But something had to happen if that boy was ever to grow up and not be possessed and smothered by love and destroyed by it. So God insists that Isaac must be sacrificed. We all know the story. They arrive at the place of sacrifice and Isaac is bound on the altar. Just as Abraham takes the knife to slay the boy, God interrupts: 'Do not kill the boy. On the contrary, he is my gift to you and the world. But at least, Abraham, you've grasped my meaning and come to the point where you could let go of him. Now you're *free*. Free at last. And so is Isaac.' (Isaac means in Hebrew, 'a joke'.)

If you think that's a crude primitive story, I can assure you that you have not lived. For it's the pattern which we all have to learn sooner or later. There's no celebration and no true enjoyment unless there is a sacrifice. Isaac is bound to the altar; the bread is put on the altar. Everything must sooner or later be brought to this point of sacrifice and freedom. For, while you hang on to life you will lose it. Let go and you will find it – and so much more besides. It is a sort of joke.

So to that Holy Communion again. He broke the bread; his heart was broken. You and I will be broken, too. It may be illness, failure, moral defeat, the loss of someone I love dearly. But see it the other way round. See it in communion with the great communion which is the great revolution. No accident is incidental. Look again and see in it the same hand that broke the bread, the same hand that was nailed to a cross, the same hand raised in a blessing. That is true freedom. That is something really worth celebrating. 'Lift up your hearts.'

The Bread of Renewal

This is the point of life: freedom. To be free to enjoy, to give and to receive the fruits of the earth, myself, others and God: for time and for eternity. What we like to call the Holy Communion is a wonderful process of change and renewal. It encapsulates the life, death and resurrection of Jesus so that what he did to that bread is the story of his life. Little wonder really then, when we stop to think about it, that he could say of the bread: 'This is my life. Take it and let it become your life: a whole way of life. And so you will find true life and true freedom.'

Take the bread; bless it; break it and give. But not the bread only. Everything. This is the destiny of the world. This is what life is all about.

> Free at last, free at last,
> Thank God Almighty, I'm free at last.

This epitaph on the tomb of Martin Luther King is the point of it all and the end-product of Holy Communion. For the Holy Communion is not simply an ecclesiastical institution which happens in your parish church every Sunday morning. Neither is it simply a pious memorial of something which happened in an upper room two thousand years ago when Jesus Christ initiated the revolution of the breaking of the bread. Rather, it is a vision of the shape of things to come as well as the shape of things as they really are, spelling out the kind of transformation that every corner of our life and world must undergo if the chrysalis of what we like to call the life of the world is to break free and be born. What he did *for* us, has got to be done *in* us – in our lives. That great saint who certainly knew what life was all about, St Augustine, said this: 'You are the body of Christ, that is to say, in you and through you the method and work of the Incarnation must go forward. You are to be taken, consecrated, broken and distributed so that you may be the means of grace and vehicles of the eternal Charity'.

His life was precisely the story of that kind of transformation and growth. But he is but one of many, many people who have found the breaking of bread a whole pattern of life which makes all the difference to life, all the difference in the world.

I can honestly say that I've seen that difference, that transformation, in ordinary people, in a congregation, in the lives of ordinary men and women, with fears and problems, limitations and hesitations. For to me the miracle is a miracle not simply about a piece of bread, but rather a miracle about life itself, as basic as the birth of a baby or the death of an old man.

Each week I turn to the congregation and say – and here's the miracle – '*We* are the Body of Christ.' That is either a sick joke or the greatest miracle of all. For the end-product is not a consecrated piece of bread, but rather men and women whose lives have been reformed and refashioned, transformed and consecrated, who can end each communion service with these daring and revolutionary words:

Almighty God, we offer thee our souls and bodies

to be a living sacrifice through Jesus Christ our Lord.
Send us out into the world in the power of thy Spirit,
to live and work to thy praise and glory.

TREVOR BEESON

The Need to Belong

The speaker on Thought for the Day sits in one of the loneliest places in the world – a radio studio. A small room almost completely cut off from the outside world. Three blank walls and on the fourth there's a glass panel through which he can see the producer and the technicians, who seem to belong to another planet. The only contact with the outside world is a microphone and a length of wire.

Now why is it, I wonder, that I feel uneasy and a little frightened? I don't think I'm afraid of broadcasting, because I've been in studios like this hundreds of times before. No, I think my uneasiness and fear is due to the fact that I'm in a situation where I don't really belong. We human beings aren't designed to be in isolation. We're designed to live in contact and relationship with other people – in community. And if we're suddenly cut off from other people we're disturbed and out of sorts.

Of course, being cut off from other people isn't simply a matter of being separated from them by walls or distance. You can be as isolated among the crowds of a great city as you can in the solitary confinement cell of a prison. When we talk about community, we're referring to the sense of belonging to other people, of being dependent upon others and responsible for others. This is the kind of people we are: 'members one of another'.

Whether we like it or not, we influence and affect one another in all kinds of ways. The mere fact that you switch on your radio in the morning means that your thoughts are turned in certain directions – possibly in unexpected directions. And as the day begins, so it continues. For the rest of your waking hours you'll be saying and doing things which influence and affect other people.

Now in this business of sharing and influencing there are all sorts of wonderful possibilities. If the communities we belong to are good ones, then our lives can be enormously enriched and we can be helped to become more happy and fulfilled. I believe that good communities are one of the chief ways in which God helps us to grow to maturity. But what do I mean by a good community? I mean a series of relationships, with individuals and groups, which provide us with stimulation and support, and help us to become more free. Most of us, I suppose, have been very grateful for the support of a community at some time or other, perhaps when we were ill or bereaved.

But, sad to say, within our ability to share and influence there are fearfully dangerous possibilities. If the communities we belong to are bad ones, then our lives can be seriously maimed and we can be reduced to frustration and despair. And by bad communities I mean those relationships – again with individuals and groups – which stifle us, which make us feel insecure, which demand more than we can give, or, worst of all, leave us on our own in our moments of deepest need. Now I don't wish to suggest that if we live in good communities we automatically become very happy and that if we live in bad ones we automatically become extremely miserable. Whatever our surroundings may be like, we still have a certain amount of freedom to respond to them. And so it's possible to live happily in bad communities and miserably in good ones. But I believe it's the task of religion – especially the Christian religion – to help to build good communities.

One of the first things Jesus did was to start a community

of twelve men who cared for each other and were convinced that they'd been called to build a new kind of world, a world in which everyone might live as a family and grow to maturity as human beings. They saw this as sharing in God's work in the world, and it's still the task of the Church today.

The Family Community

For most of us the basic community to which we belong is the family. This is the group into which we were born. It provides the situation in which we have our most intimate relationships and where we spend some of our happiest moments. What is more, family life is still extremely popular. In spite of all the talk about changing moral standards and so forth, marriage is still very much with us.

Why is this? Chiefly, I believe, because the deep relationships expressed in family life give us a setting in which we feel secure, emotionally and physically, and because we're secure we're free to be ourselves – for better or for worse. These are the conditions we need if we're to grow in the best possible way.

Some of the best family communities I know are those in which the husband and wife sometimes have the most almighty rows. The fur really does fly, and there's a lot of pain, but everything's all right because there's deep commitment and trust underneath; in fact the commitment and trust allow the anger to emerge. On the other hand, some of the most unsatisfactory family communities I know are those in which a cross word is rarely, if ever, spoken; the commitment and trust don't run deep enough to allow the risk of anger being taken.

What is important for husbands and wives is equally so for children. A good family community is one in which a child can be himself, in which he can express his feelings and emotions and needs without fear of rejection. Those of us who are parents sometimes get anxious when our young children fly into tantrums or our teenagers go berserk. But when this happens it's worth asking ourselves: Where else in the world can this child or this young person feel free to express these important emotions in this way? Of course, freedom doesn't imply an undisciplined and destructive free-for-all. Membership of any community involves accepting responsibility for others, something which adults as well as children are constantly required to relearn in the family setting.

So far, I've been trying to share with you some thoughts on the creative possibilities of family life. But I'm afraid there's another side to this coin. If the family's the place where some experience their greatest happiness, it's also the place where some experience their most devastating pain and anguish. If there isn't sufficient commitment and trust, the family community is built on insecurity, and the closeness involved in living together under the same roof simply heightens the sense of disorder.

Now what is it that makes the difference between a creative and a destructive family community? I believe the difference lies in the presence or absence of real love. And when I say love I'm not referring primarily to the romantic side of love (though I think that's very important); I'm thinking of that self-giving and accepting love which belongs to the very centre of our lives and which makes us the kind of people we are. For me, this love is the clearest evidence for, and expression of, the presence of God – the God whose life fills our inmost being and who's working constantly for our good. Married love can be one of the most powerful channels of God's love; through the family he shows his concern for us and gives himself to us.

Several points about family life seem to me to flow from this:

1. Praise and blame aren't words which can properly be used in a marriage. When love expresses itself in commitment and trust we can be thankful; when it doesn't we can only be sorry.
2. The ability to love, or to be loved by, a particular person is largely outside our control. We can only respond to what is given to us.
3. Because relationships are living things, they have within themselves the possibility of change – of deepening or of weakening. And this is as true within the family community as it is outside it.
4. Within the family community, law is of very limited usefulness. It may give formal expression to what is; it cannot create or maintain what isn't.
5. Whatever the condition of our family community, there's always the possibility of something good emerging for as long as we accept responsibility towards those who share our life and our love.

The Neighbourhood Community

The Hertfordshire town where I live is more than a thousand years old. It has about 15,000 people and a very good cross-section of English society. It can take hours to walk down the ancient High Street, especially on market day, because one is always bumping into people one knows and the time of day is passed or a question raised with an urban district councillor. It's that kind of place, friendly, accepting. I don't think any of us would pretend that it's heaven on earth, but it's a jolly good community.

Unfortunately, not every neighbourhood is like ours. I think, for example, of some of the housing estates in South London which consist almost entirely of huge blocks of flats. It's interesting that if you build a street vertically instead of horizontally you do something to the people who live in it. Instead of feeling that you belong, you feel desperately isolated. You never meet any of your neighbours, except when you're cooped up in a lift with them for a few seconds. You could be ill – or even dead – for weeks without anyone ever knowing. The scale of the place is threatening, not accepting. Instead of providing stimulation, estates of this kind often cause deep depression; instead of offering support, they only expose and aggravate weakness.

Between these extremes – the country town and the high-rise estate – there are of course many variations. And these variations are important because we know that the quality of neighbourhood life has a great influence on the personal happiness and the behaviour of individuals. It is no accident that educational attainment is high in a prosperous, well-knit town like my own. It's not just a coincidence that crime and delinquency are most common in the run-down areas of our large cities. And no one who's lived in a large new housing area will be a bit surprised to hear that the suicide rate in such areas is well above the national average. A neighbourhood can be life-enhancing and creative or it can be death-dealing and destructive.

In view of this it's surely surprising how little attention the planners seem to give to neighbourhood needs when building new estates or destroying old towns. All too often it's supposed that as long as we put a decent roof over a family's head, we've done all that needs to be done. But this isn't so. Human beings need an environment in which they can easily relate to others outside the family circle. I always think it's significant that the Bible begins with the story of two people in a garden and ends with the vision of a great city – the perfect community. In this way it highlights a basic Christian belief that God works in and through men and women as they build, and become part of, real communities.

Neighbourhood and community is, however, a rather complex matter these days. For most of its thousand years of history, the community life of my own town could be symbolised by a cartwheel. Until 150 years or so ago, the people spent every part of their life – their work, their play, their homes, their friendships – within the town's boundaries. The old parish church at the centre was a kind of hub to which everyone and everything related like spokes in a wheel. It was possible to speak of a single, united community.

But things are different now. Most of us belong to a series of different communities, and we go to different places and relate to different people for the various elements which make up our personal and community life. Quite often, considerable distances separate home from work, school from recreation. And so the appropriate symbol for community life today is not a cartwheel but a series of interlocking cogs.

The question we have to face then is: How can we keep these cogs moving together, so that they can develop all their creative possibilities for individuals and for neighbourhoods as a whole? The answer calls for a good deal of social skill and sensitivity. I believe it also raises some serious religious questions about the nature and needs of man – the remarkable being who's made to belong, and whose happiness and fulfilment, and whose response to God, depends so much on his relationships with others.

The Working Community

I wonder how many of you look forward to going to work each morning? Quite a lot, I imagine, because work is a place where you express a very important part of your being – your creativity. Furthermore, it's a place where you enjoy a number of very rewarding relationships – with your colleagues, and possibly with lots of other people as well.

But I know that a very large number of you don't look forward to those eight working hours in your life. You'd give anything to be able to stay at home, or at least to do something different, because your job is a boring drudgery. It involves only a tiny fraction of your creative ability.

Then, as if this were not bad enough in itself, there are the actual working conditions you have to face. You feel that you're caught up in a system which is ruthless and basically inhuman. You feel that far from being important as a person, you are only a small cog in a vast, impersonal machine. No wonder you don't feel like going to work.

And we ought to be clear that there's nothing wrong in not wanting to go to work. There was a time – not so long ago – when religion tried to hold up work as something good in itself; something you had to do in order to be a responsible, integrated person. But this was a mistake and it led to a good deal of exploitation. The real Christian insight is not that we're obliged to go to an office or a factory, but that we're designed to be creative; we're all meant to share in some way in that process of continuous creation which keeps our universe in being and makes it such a wonderful place in which to be. And there's a two-way traffic in this because as we become creative we become more open to the creative power of God. An old monk once said that he felt as near to God while he was washing up in the monastery kitchen as he did while kneeling in the chapel at Mass.

But in our present world-order most of us have very little choice in the matter. It's necessary for us to put in an appearance at a particular place and to do a certain job simply in order to survive. As things are, you can't live on creativity;

only on wage packets. And it is, I believe, a clear sign of the disorder of our society that for so many people such a wide gulf exists between their need to be creative and their need to earn enough to live on. When industrialists and trade union leaders turn their minds in this direction, we shall know that at long last they've decided to deal with the causes, rather than the symptoms, of our industrial disease.

In the meantime, certain things have to be asserted and, where possible, translated into practice. If our working communities are to become more creative and less destructive for those involved in them, certain priorities have to be established. I mention two:

Persons must come before profits.

Relationships must come before things.

In any working unit – whether it be a factory or an office, a shop or a school – the well-being of those who are actually engaged in the activity has the first claim upon the management and the money. After all, the people involved are human beings who are devoting a large slice of their life to a particular job. If their legitimate interests are regarded as less important than balance sheets or markets they are dehumanised and, in the long run, they won't be able to make their best contribution to the whole enterprise. In the same way, if relationships between people at work are made secondary to machinery and efficiency a further dehumanisation takes place; and, again, the consequences for individuals and for the enterprise are likely to be destructive.

This isn't an argument for smashing machines and returning to cottage industries. It's simply a plea that in all the complex changes now taking place on the working scene, we should recognise who we're dealing with. A human being is not that part of a machine or system which has yet to be invented, but a person with deep needs – the need to create, the need to belong. And the creation of the humane society –

and therefore an efficient society – demands that these deep needs shall be respected.

The Church Community

In my reflections on our need for community, I've made very few comments which you could identify as specifically religious. Yet we've been involved in a series of religious reflections because community is to do with the nature of man and so with the meeting of certain deep needs: the need to belong, the need for stimulus and support, the need to become free.

Now in the broad sense you may accept this – or at least concede it as a possibility. But I wouldn't be a bit surprised if you were to ask me what all this has got to do with that funny old church round the corner. I often wonder myself!

Churches are strange places. Their architecture may be very beautiful, but the people who go to them indulge in some unusual practices. All of which can be a bit off-putting. But behind the externals, there's always a group of people (sometimes a handful, sometimes several hundreds) who are trying to become a community. They're reaching out to belong, to find acceptance and support, to receive insight, to express themselves as beings created in the image and likeness of God.

At their best these church communities are exceedingly creative. Within their strange rituals and meetings and activities they offer certain people a situation in which they are accepted and loved and encouraged and illuminated. If you go to a Baptism or to Communion, for example, you find yourself caught up in a kind of family atmosphere, welcoming new arrivals, sharing in a meal. Both of these occasions help people to grow, to become more mature by their involvement in the life of a community.

In Britain alone there are over 50,000 such church communities functioning today. And the overwhelming majority of them aren't merely concerned with providing comforts for their own members; they reach out into all kinds of social activity in the neighbourhoods around them. The churches – for all their failings – contribute far more to the well-being of individuals and local communities and the nation as a whole than is commonly recognised.

'For all their failings'. Not all church communities are good and creative. Some of them are exceedingly bad and very destructive. It's a curious fact of human life that when something which is basically good becomes corrupted, its power and drive often creates appalling havoc. Those of us who know the churches well have seen individuals tortured and destroyed by the corrupt working of ecclesiastical machinery. Those of us who belong to the Church are saddened, but perhaps not altogether surprised, because we recognise the same destructive tendencies within ourselves.

Wherein lies the difference, then, between the Church and any other expression of human community? I suggest two distinctive points: one is to do with the Church's origins, the other with its particular insights.

The Church was brought into being by Jesus of Nazareth in order to provide the human race with a model of what life in community is really like. The kind of things we've been thinking about this week – belonging and caring and accepting and growing – constitute the basic core of the teaching of Jesus. But he was concerned to leave us with more than a string of sayings and sermons on the subject of community. He aimed to give us the living example of an actual community in which these creative qualities are being lived out. The Church is this model. Which isn't to say, of course, that the world ought to be like the Church in all the detailed aspects of its life. It is to say that the Church is an example of human beings in relationship – of community – and that this example should be translatable in every area of human life and experience.

And because the Church owes its origin to Jesus of Nazareth, it is, in its quest for community, driven to look deep and wide. The Church knows that the creation of true community isn't simply a matter of social engineering (though this requires far more careful attention than it normally receives) but calls for insight into the meaning of life itself. Community health, like personal health, is a by-product of something else – of a life which responds to that burning love which is at the heart of reality and which makes us 'members one of another' in the family of man, which is also the family of God.

MICHAEL TAYLOR

Costly Grace

Dietrich Bonhoeffer was executed in Germany in 1945. He was hanged not from a cross like his Lord but from a rope. He will long be remembered as a Christian martyr. It was Bonhoeffer who coined the phrase 'costly grace' in a little book called *The Cost of Discipleship* written some years before he died. In the light of subsequent events his remarks have about them the ring of truth. It did indeed turn out to be an expensive business. Nevertheless, 'costly grace' is a strange idea when you stop to think about it, almost amounting to a contradiction in terms.

'Grace' is a big word, capable of endless definition, but whatever its exact meaning we usually think of it as a gift. The 'means of grace' are ways in which the gift or gifts are received, and when we talk about God as gracious we are referring to his generosity. But aren't we right to assume that gifts are free? The giver may have to pay quite handsomely, whether he gives a birthday present or something less tangible like forgiveness or loyalty. Giving such things may cost a great deal, but you don't expect to be involved in a lot of expense at the receiving end! A gift you pay for ceases to qualify as a gift at all. It has been bought at a price.

Talk about 'costly grace' sounds curious, to say the least. Perhaps we can understand it a little better if we remember that not all gifts are alike and they are not all received in the same way.

Take for example the presents we give each other at birthdays or Christmas or at a wedding. We certainly don't expect to pay for them. It's a fairly undemanding sort of exchange. Like laughter and sunshine these gifts are there for the taking and ask no more of us than that we accept and enjoy them.

It's a different story if the gift is a new baby in the family, or an unexpected chance to do the kind of job you've always wanted to do. The baby must be brought up properly. You must seize your chance and make the most of the new job. Some gifts do carry responsibilities. The world of nature and the resources of the earth are gifts which all of us freely inherit, but we must take care of them, maybe rather better than we have done in the past. There is a price to pay.

But take yet another example. I'm not at all exceptional in wanting the best for my children, or in realising now and again that the best is not to be calculated in terms of fame and fortune. I want them to have treasure like patience and courage, compassion, modesty, good judgement and wide sympathies. But how do I give them and how are they ever received? We know very well that such things are not simply handed over like boxes of sweets or birthday presents, and they are not so much demanding when you've got them as demanding to get in the first place. They are only to be had in the hard school of life by making an effort, going on adventures, suffering bravely, making mistakes, being vulnerable, getting hurt and learning to forgive. If our children are ever to receive the kind of maturity we would like them to have, we shall have to make it costly for them as well as for us.

We can talk about the grace or generosity of God in all the ways I've mentioned and no doubt many more, but it's this last one which comes close to the heart of the matter. God is like a father who wants his children to grow up to become the best they have it in them to be; and it is because his grace is that kind of a gift that it is costly. You cannot have maturity on the cheap. We could even say that the cost of grace is the only possible means of grace. There is no inexpensive way by which maturity can be given or received.

Following Jesus

As Bonhoeffer implied, the cost of grace is the cost of discipleship. We grow up to maturity – or find salvation, if you like – by following Jesus of Nazareth. That sounds like a fairly simple idea until we begin to ask what it means in practice. It cannot mean what it meant to the twelve men who were first invited to follow. We cannot go with Jesus to Galilee or the wilderness or down the Jericho road or through the streets of Jerusalem. People do talk about his presence with us now, but it cannot be anything like enjoying his company then.

Since we cannot actually follow him, is the alternative to follow his example? We cannot go where Jesus went, but we can try and do as Jesus did. On reflection that's not a very practical idea either, and in some cases it may not be a very good one. Even if we could know exactly what Jesus did, should we necessarily want to do the same? As a genuine human being he had his limitations and no doubt made his mistakes. We should want to learn from them and overcome them, not merely repeat them.

But the most serious objection to copying Christ's example is that for much of the time there is no example to copy. Whole tracts of our experience scarcely receive a mention. It seems unlikely that Jesus was married for example, and even less likely that he had children. If he did, he has virtually nothing to say about what for most of us amounts to a pretty significant slice of life; and what he does say is said against a background very different from our own. Families seem to have been exceptionally close in his day, so much so that Jesus drops broad hints about the need to break them up a bit. There are other things to consider besides family loyalty. Few of us will readily follow that advice. More likely we shall note how times have changed so that far from breaking it up, we are frequently urged to get together a bit more!

This distance between Jesus and ourselves could be illustrated over and over again. His example isn't all that helpful and on many occasions it appears to be almost totally irrelevant. It is tempting to make a list of some of the issues that repeatedly bother us in our industrial, political and economic life, and ask: 'What has Jesus to say about that?' Nine times out of ten the answer will be: 'Nothing!' mainly because the issues we face did not confront him, and our world is not his world.

Of course we can take that too far. We certainly live in two different worlds, but they are often recognisably the same. As we read the Gospels we come across people like ourselves and a humanity we know all too well. If we didn't we should have to conclude that Jesus had nothing to do with us at all, and that would be a mistake.

But it is equally mistaken – and this is what I've been trying to make clear – to expect too much from Jesus in terms of detailed advice. Discipleship cannot mean having eyes only for him. Much of what we learn as we grow towards maturity will not be derived directly from Jesus of Nazareth but from the people and the traditions which surround us here and now, and the welcome and not so welcome experiences of life. This is what we should expect if we see life as a means of grace, filled by a generous God with creative opportunities to help us become what we are meant to be.

In so far as Jesus is a guide to follow, he does not offer exhaustive descriptions of the route but revealing hints as to the best general direction to take. In deciding what we have to do he cannot be the only consideration, though for Christians he remains the most important one to bear in mind. The result of taking him seriously is not a set of answers which preclude all discussion, but an ongoing dialogue in which we are expected to answer back and required like growing adults to think for ourselves. Discipleship is not for copy-cats since we do not learn maturity by rote.

To the Outside

Reading the story of Jesus it is difficult to escape the suggestion that our maturity is best achieved by forgetting about it and working with others to achieve theirs. When I wonder where to start I find at least a question mark placed against the conventional wisdom that charity begins at home. Jesus does not strike me as unmindful of domestic responsibilities, but appearing throughout the Gospel narratives is a motley collection of what can only be described as rank outsiders.

Let me list one or two of them: a tax collector, by the name of Zacchaeus, who worked for the Roman occupying forces and who today would be dubbed a quisling; a pitiful creature calling himself Legion, living in a graveyard and probably driven insane by the brutalities of war; a woman who barged in on a highly respectable dinner party with doubtful credentials; a Samaritan whom few if any would lift a finger to help; a common thief about to hang for his crimes; a Gentile, definitely regarded as not one of us; and perhaps most isolated of all, a leper safely kept clear of all human contact. And these are not the only ones to claim and win the attention of Jesus.

Perhaps one aspect of discipleship is to follow Christ *there*, to these frayed edges of our life together. Again that is no more than a hint or a sense of direction. It offers no simple formula for recognising an outsider, let alone what to do when we see one. Now as then not all are outside for the same reason. Some are unpopular. Some are regarded as dangerous and best put away. Others are the objects of disapproval or prejudice or fear. One or two are thought to deserve all that they get. Some have little more than nuisance value, conveniently forgotten and left to nurse their own troubles. Outsiders have very little in common.

We must also remember that times have changed. We are probably more tolerant than the contemporaries of Jesus of a wider spectrum of moral behaviour, and we have learnt to deal with what were once terrifying diseases so that we are no longer afraid. As a result, some of the outsiders of his day are now in; others like the deprived and forgotten, the poor, the prisoners and the victims of prejudice are still out. And when we look round our world and our cities, these at least are not difficult to see.

One could hope that our reasons for getting involved with them would be no more pretentious than straightforward compassion and human friendliness. But in a self-conscious age like ours it is difficult to strike the right note and avoid the kind of condescension which suggests that we are the only ones who have anything to give, and that we are dealing with out inferiors rather than our equals. Such approaches have convinced many outsiders that they are better left alone to help themselves.

Respect for other people's feelings need not however

result in paralysis. We should be prepared to give what we can where people find it acceptable, but we must be even more prepared to receive and to learn at the same time. I am not now advocating the dewy-eyed romanticism which regards outsiders as all good and insiders as all bad. We are one another's equals, good and bad alike. I am suggesting that outsiders can tell us a great deal about ourselves.

Why do we cast them out or leave them out? The answers to such questions can be very revealing about what we find acceptable and what we don't, about our prejudices and our fears, about the things that hurt us or shame us and which we would rather forget.

Following Christ to the outsider is primarily a journey of compassion, but it is also an exercise in growing self-awareness. To know ourselves a little better is not usually a very pleasant experience. It may prove to be as disturbing for us as it was for Jews in the time of Jesus when again and again an outsider brought to their attention aspects of themselves they preferred to ignore. But coming to terms with the unacceptable face of oneself is one of the ways to maturity; which only illustrates how the cost of discipleship and the means of grace are two aspects of a single reality.

To the Inside

Most of us will readily admit that someone coming fresh to a problem can often see things more clearly than those who've been involved in it for a long time. But in the end it is the person who knows the details really well who can be of most help.

Jesus of Nazareth was such a person, thoroughly familiar with the situation in Palestine under the Romans. He knew the various schools of thought, political and religious, from the collaborators to those with bloody revolution running in their veins. He knew all about the burdens of the Jew – his moral integrity and crushed national pride. He was well aware of the hopes being nursed and the kind of leader they were looking for. And when he dealt with individuals, whether they were top brass or the little people of the land, he apparently understood what life was like for them. As a result, he seems to know what most needs to be done, and when he speaks he invariably hits the nail on the head. If it is usually inappropriate for us to say and do the same things as he did, it is mainly because they were so exactly right and fitting at the time. Jesus does what you might call an inside job because it can only be pulled off with inside information.

If one aspect of discipleship is to follow him to the outside, is another to follow him in a rather different sense to the inside as well? That will require a good deal of patience. Of course we all know important areas of life from the inside already, and maybe we should take them more seriously than we do. How often do we hive off and deal with things superficially elsewhere instead of trying to cope responsibly where we are. To that extent we ought to begin at home as Jesus begins with his own house of Israel.

But in so far as we go into more unfamiliar territory, there are no short cuts to the point where we can be of real use. The ins and outs of first-century Jewish affairs apparently took thirty years of knowing by a young man who was unusually perceptive. How much more is that true of us and the complex issues of today. If we are to make a relevant contribution to a more human and grown-up world, there is a lot to learn before we venture to speak; and the ill-informed had better be silent.

When it comes to the personal level, an even greater reticence may be called for. However good our intentions we have no right to barge in on other people's lives. We can only go where we are invited and we may have to wait a very long time – perhaps for ever – before they see sufficient reason to extend an invitation.

Once inside we must tread with the greatest care and courtesy, and this is where the most painful reassessments will have to begin. As disciples we believe we have seen in Jesus the way, the truth and the life for every man. The result is a great temptation to go to people with pre-packaged gospels and panaceas, equally suited to very occasion. We have ready-made answers before we have even heard the questions. If we are patient enough to listen, the inner realities of people's lives will soon bring home to us that our easy generalities won't do. They are too highly polished to come to grips with anything that matters. We shall have to break them down and struggle again and again to discover what has to be done and said in this particular set of circumstances. As with Jesus, so with us: what saves and heals on one occasion will not necessarily save or heal on another. It is a discovery not a foregone conclusion, and it can only be made on the inside.

But many of these qualities we've been talking about – like patience and reticence, the ability to think again and the readiness not to impose solutions but make a genuine response – many of these qualities are generally regarded as marks of maturity. What discipleship requires, a growing maturity will increasingly possess. What is demanded of us and given to us are inextricably bound together. Cost and grace are hand in glove.

To the Cross

Of all the aspects of discipleship we could talk about – and we have only mentioned a few – perhaps the most striking has to do with the cross. It is stated quite categorically: 'If anyone wishes to be a follower of mine . . . day after day he must take up his cross and come with me.' That is worrying as well as striking since the majority of us come nowhere near to crucifixion.

Of course life has its ups and downs and we all have our crosses to bear, but it is one thing to shoulder them when you have no choice, it is quite another to pick one up of your own free will. We all suffer from time to time but most of us would be hard put to it to say we ever suffer as disciples. If we do, we have to admit it is on a comparatively trivial level. Men have literally followed Christ to a martyr's death and still do, but we are left only to complain that it isn't easy to be a Christian these days or, by way of excuse, to point out that there is more than one way to suffer. On the whole the mild embarrassments we put up with do little to qualify our comfort or, if we are really disturbed by the cross of Christ, to alleviate our guilt.

Nevertheless we must be clear about one thing. Crucifixion is not to be sought for its own sake. We do not become disciples by making martyrs of ourselves. It is discipleship that must make martyrs of us. The cross which has become so central is really incidental. It is not the object of the journey. It is shouldered on the way.

For example, as we follow Christ to the outside edges of our life together and become good companions of those who suffer as the objects of other men's fears and disapproval, prejudice or dislike, the same antagonistic feelings will no doubt be transferred to us. Those who go after outsiders run the risk of being edged out themselves. The martyr of Calvary finds himself outside the walls of the city, outside the law and apparently outside the immediate concerns of his own followers as he is left alone to die.

And as we follow Christ to the inside of human life, patiently listening and learning and trying to understand, one result is almost bound to be sympathy of the very best kind, when we not only feel for but feel with a fellow human being. At Calvary Jesus of Nazareth is not only the victim who suffers at the hands of other men, he is also our friend and brother who has entered deeply into the pains of our human experience.

Either way, crosses by themselves are not the hallmark of discipleship, but its consequence.

Finally, perhaps we should return to the curious paradox with which we began: the cost of discipleship, even when it becomes as alarmingly expensive as this, is in fact the means of grace. It is the way by which we gain our maturity and are made whole and complete. 'Whoever cares for his own safety is lost; but if a man will let himself be lost for my sake that man is safe.'

I haven't any convincing evidence to support this strange suggestion that just when everything seems to have been thrown away everything may well have been found. I can only point to those costly and testing experiences of life when we feel like the losers but from which now and again we unexpectedly gain so much. I can also point to the heart of the Christian vision which illuminates those very experiences. At the cross and resurrection of Jesus a man quite literally lets himself be lost only to find himself again, transformed into a glory undreamed of before. By way of the pleasure and pain of life with its constant demands, its mistakes and its limitations, he is brought to his most destructive moment which turns out to be his most creative. Loser takes all. He is made complete. Christ is risen, the first of the harvest of the dead, to remain for many of us the hope that all our dying will not ultimately be the breaking of us but the making of our humanity.